25.00

ROSES

for the
Scented Room

BARBARA MILO OHRBACH

ROSES

for the Scented Room

Beautiful Ideas
for Entertaining,
Gift-giving
and the Home

PHOTOGRAPHS BY JOHN HALL

CLARKSON POTTER/PUBLISHERS NEW YORK

AUTHOR'S NOTE: This book contains recipes using botanicals and other natural ingredients. Some of these may cause allergic reactions in some individuals, so reasonable care in preparation is advised.

Published by Clarkson Potter/Publishers
201 East 50th Street
New York, New York 10022
Member of the Crown Publishing Group

Random House, Inc. New York, Toronto, London, Sydney, Auckland
www.randomhouse.com

CLARKSON N. POTTER, POTTER, and colophon are registered trademarks of Random House, Inc.

Printed in China

Design by Dania Davey and Lisa Sloane

Library of Congress
Cataloging-in-Publication Data
Ohrbach, Barbara Milo.
   Roses for the scented room : beautiful ideas for entertaining, gift-giving and the home / Barbara Milo Ohrbach : photographs by John Hall. — 1st ed.
   Includes bibliographical references.
   1. Nature craft.   2. Roses.   I. Title.
TT157.038   2000
745.5—dc21   99-32988
                                                            CIP

ISBN 0-609-60107-5

10   9   8   7   6   5   4   3   2   1

First Edition

For Dad

ACKNOWLEDGMENTS

"Just living is not enough, said the butterfly.
One must have sunshine, freedom, and a little flower."

My special gratitude to everyone listed below for their inspiration and help on this book—especially John Hall, Dania Martinez Davey, Deborah Geltman, Gayle Benderoff and Mel Ohrbach, who worked so hard to make this book happen. Thank you to all my friends at Clarkson Potter: Annetta Hanna, my wonderful editor; her terrific assistant, John Son; the ever-talented Jane Treuhaft; and Leigh Ann Ambrosi, Amy Boorstein, Paula Cohen, Joan Denman, Chip Gibson, Debbie Koenig, Teresa Nicholas, Elaine Panagides, Andrea Connolly Peabbles, Mary Sarah Quinn, Christian Red, Wendy Schuman, Lauren Shakely, Lisa Sloane, Laurie Stark, Robin Strashun, Rebecca Strong and June Zimmerman.

Thank you for sharing gracious hospitality and beauty with me: Antonia Bakker-Salvato, Nicola Blazier, Susan Branch and Scalamandré Fabrics, Andrée Brunet, Christina J. Deeny, Irene Devine, Gudren Engl, Pierre Ferchaud, Doris Goddard, Pat Griffiths, Gerald Hardy, Kathrin Hess, Mary Homi, Gilbert Irondelle, Pauline Jones, Victoria King, Jeff Lark, Herbert Laubichler-Pichler, Peter MacCann, William Mihans, Karyn Millet, Ruth Moran, Valerie Muller, Thierry Naidu, Mary O'Keefe, Gianni Riatsch, Roberto Scio, Thelma Sears, John Shore, Margareta Siegel-Callahan, Brigitte and Martin Skan, Donna Smith, Julia Sweeney, Roger Vergé, Maria and Peter Warren, Carmen, Peter and Roberto Wirth and Gabriele Wolf.

My appreciation to the following for their photographs used in Chapter 10: Andrew Lawson, English Gardens; Karyn Millet and the Merrion Hotel, Irish details; Larry Albee, Longwood Gardens; and to Hans Christian Andersen for the wonderful quote above.

TABLE OF CONTENTS

A Rose Is Best

Celebrating with Roses

Everything's Coming Up Roses

Of all flowers,

methinks

a

rose

is best.

William Shakespeare

INTRODUCTION

Roses. What could be more perfect than a flower that comes in almost every exquisite color imaginable, a flower whose alluring fragrance is a key ingredient in the world's most famous perfumes and whose sublime beauty has made it the ultimate accolade. There's no finer compliment than having a rose named after you—an honor accorded to Elizabeth Taylor, John F. Kennedy, Queen Elizabeth, Cary Grant and Grace Kelly, among others.

As a teenager I adored Grace Kelly, and I put together a scrapbook based on her storybook wedding. I was thrilled many years later when she visited my shop, Cherchez, and when I discovered that she loved flowers, and roses in particular. It was then that I bought her book, in which she wrote, "What is so special about a rose, that it seems far more than a flower? Perhaps it is the mystery it has gathered through the ages. Perhaps it is the joy that it continues to give."

Since roses were first discovered, people have been passionate about them. Today they are more popular than ever. This may be because beauty has never been more essential. We all live fast-paced lives and often need to soften the impact of our busy schedules. There seem to be fewer and fewer beautiful things in a world becoming less and less attractive. So why not focus on something beautiful that gives us joy, like roses?

My fascination with them began with my high school prom, when I received my first rose corsage. Later, when I married, my husband and I planned our first rose garden at our new house in the country. Looking through the rose catalogues was a wonderful experience—such luscious photographs, such intriguing names. And then when the roses were actually in bloom, their fragrance was more beautiful than anything we could have imagined.

By now, roses have become old friends to me. They are everywhere I look in our home—embroidered on textiles, painted on porcelain plates, hand-colored in old engravings. When I look out the window, they are there too—climbing gloriously over trellises, walls and arbors.

And, as you will read later in this book, our travels are influenced by roses too. On a trip to the South of France, we visited Grasse to enjoy the treasures in Fragonard's Perfume Museum and to buy fragrance and rose-scented soaps. We nestled in at the sumptuous Domaine St. Martin, serene in the hills above Vence, where roses grow everywhere. The next day we had a memorable lunch in the garden of Roger Vergé's charming restaurant in Mougins, which included a dessert made with rose petal syrup.

On our way back to Paris, we stopped in at one of our favorite gardens, Villandry, on the banks of the Loire, whose owner continues the generations-old practice of planting color-coordinated vegetables in rose-edged parterres.

We have been living with roses for a long time, and they've enhanced every facet of our lives. I first wrote about them in *The Scented Room,* where I confessed my love of the old-fashioned varieties that were then just coming back into popularity. *A Token of*

PREVIOUS PAGE: A wood artist model on my desk holds a bouquet of small Fairy roses.

OPPOSITE, CLOCKWISE: Roses are a favorite motif of mine. Here, Le Moulin de Mougins, where we had our dessert served on rose-painted plates; a collection of my porcelain dishes; and my eighteenth-century embroidered vests.

Friendship, published soon after, was a result of my collecting antique watercolors and engravings of flowers. My books *Simply Flowers* and *Antiques At Home* feature many beautiful old objects decorated with roses. I'm on book number sixteen now, and roses still weave in and out of everything I set my mind to.

Roses from the Scented Room is filled with great ideas for rose lovers. It starts off with interesting historical facts and clarifies the sometimes confusing categories of roses. The two chapters that follow tell you what to look for when choosing roses and include tips for making them last longer and for drying them. Chapters 4 and 5 are filled with imaginative ideas for making gifts like aromatherapy oils and for cooking with roses. Chapter 6 tells you what to do with the beautiful bouquet you just received. And Chapters 7 and 8 are about turning dried roses into wonderfully scented sachets and other projects. The next chapter, "Entertaining," features unusual ideas for weddings and parties, like making a rose ice bucket and rose confetti.

Since I love traveling, and know you do too, I've listed some of my favorite rose gardens in Chapter 10, plus other outstanding places I've encountered along the way. The "Source Guide" lists insider garden tours, special rose books, organizations to join, and where to buy rose bushes and some of the items featured in this book.

For many years roses have fed my soul. So what could be more natural than to write a book about them? I have loved working on it and hope that as you turn the pages, you'll enjoy walking in my footsteps. As Eleanor Perenyi said in her book *Green Thoughts,* "When it comes to roses some of us are incurable."

Barbara Milo Ohrbach

ABOVE: This restored building in Vienna was designed in 1898 by the famous architect Otto Wagner.
OPPOSITE: Roses gracefully climbing the olive trees at Hotel Château du Domaine St.-Martin in France.

A ROSE

Lizzie

Wishing you
Many Happy Returns
of the Day

IS A ROSE

Oh! No man knows through what wild centuries roves back the rose.

Walter de la Mare

ALL ABOUT ROSES

Roses have been part of the landscape from the very earliest times. Fossilized roses found in the western United States are said to have bloomed millions of years ago. And once humans appeared, roses began to weave in and out of our history.

Greek mythology is filled with lush images of the flower; Homer, for example, talks about the "rosy-fingered dawn." Aphrodite, the goddess of love, chose roses as her personal symbol—perhaps one reason why the fortunate among us receive a dozen of them on Valentine's Day. The Romans used roses so lavishly that the poet Horace complained that too many were being grown in Italy, and not enough corn! And in thousand-year-old Chinese paintings, we can still identify some of the roses illustrated.

Crusaders returning to England from exotic places like the Middle East brought back rose cuttings. In the fifteenth century, the Tudor Rose, a white rose placed in the center of a red rose, became the emblem of the British monarchy, signifying a national reconciliation after the famous War of the Roses.

Around the same time in France, images of roses were woven into the Unicorn Tapestries. Later, Madame de Pompadour, the mistress of Louis XV, loved roses so much that she carried them wherever she went. She had rose garlands sewn into the hems of her gowns and was often painted holding the lovely rose "Belle de Crécy," which many of us have growing in our gardens today.

Napoleon's wife, Empress Josephine, was also an ardent collector of roses. In fact, a temporary truce was declared at the height of the Napoleonic Wars so that a rare tea rose could be safely delivered to her. Painter Pierre-Joseph Redouté recorded her roses at Malmaison, creating a folio of 169 elegant varieties in exquisite watercolors; this resulted in him being called the "Raphael of roses."

Rose cuttings were nurtured like babies by pioneer women during their rough wagon trips to the American West. In the nineteenth century, Queen Victoria and her subjects adored roses in their gardens, and the first National Rose Show was held in London in 1858. At the turn of the century, Scottish Arts and Crafts designer Charles Rennie Mackintosh included roses into his decorative work and architecture, as did designers of the Vienna Secessionist school.

Fragonard, Monet, Renoir, Fantin-Latour, Shelley, Tennyson, Burns and Wilde are just a few of the many artists and writers who were inspired by the beauty of roses. There are endless intriguing facts about them, some of which I can't resist adding here:

🌹 Peter Carl Fabergé, the Russian imperial jeweler, kept roses in a hothouse above his Moscow shop so that he could study them all year round and re-create their exact flowering.

🌹 Shakespeare mentioned the rose more than sixty times, almost always to symbolize perfection.

🌹 It took two full days to pick the many roses at Mount Vernon, George Washington's plantation.

🌹 When a secret meeting was to be held in ancient Rome, a garland of roses was hung over the door—hence the term "sub rosa."

🌹 The perforated spout of a watering can is often called a rose.

One of the types of full moons is called a Rose Moon.

The last plane to leave France for the United States in 1940, just ahead of the German army, carried the cuttings of a new rose developed by the distinguished Meilland Nurseries. It flourished, and when the war was over, it became known throughout the world as the "Peace Rose," the most famous of its generation.

Today there are approximately 20,000 varieties of roses in almost every imaginable shape, size and color. This may sound confusing, but it isn't if you keep in mind that most of them fall into the following groups:

Wild or Species Roses

These roses first appeared thousands of years ago. Generally found in the wild, they are the ancestors of the garden roses we see today. They usually have single flowers with five petals and rose hips. Most are hearty, resistant to disease and require little maintenance, hence their longevity.

PAGE 17: I found this silver medallion in the Nice antiques market.

OPPOSITE: Roses chain-stitched on the corner of a treasured shawl from my collection of antique textiles.
RIGHT: A rose saves my place in an old book, *Rapin of Gardens*, written in 1706.

Old Garden Roses

Sometimes called old-fashioned roses, these varieties were in existence before 1867. Their characteristics include a lavish growing habit, soft colors ranging from white to deepest pink and the headiest fragrance imaginable. They are easy to grow and tolerant of neglect. There are approximately eleven types of old garden roses, divided into two groups: those that bloom only once a year and are single-flowering (called pre-China), and those called repeat bloomers, which bloom all season long.

Single-Flowering

Gallica The *Rosa gallica* was cultivated in medieval times in most monastery gardens; it is sometimes called the apothecary rose.

Damask Originally from Damascus, Syria, this rose is known for its long history and strong fragrance. Kazanlik is a variety that has been grown for centuries in Bulgaria for attar of roses, the precious oil used to make expensive perfumes.

Alba This elegant rose is often found in Italian Renaissance paintings.

Centifolia Known as the cabbage rose because of its many-leafed blossom, it was first produced by the Dutch in the sixteenth century.

Moss This balsam-scented old rose has a mosslike covering on the stems that is sticky to the touch.

Repeat-Flowering

China roses These roses were introduced to the West from China in 1781. They caused a great sensation because they blossomed not once a year, but repeatedly all summer long. They were bred with European roses, resulting in the following varieties:

• **Portland** This rose is said to have first appeared in the eighteenth-century English garden of the second Duchess of Portland.

• **Bourbon** With a fragrance that is reminiscent of apples, this rose emerged in the nineteenth century.

• **Hybrid Perpetual** A favorite of the Victorians, this was the precursor of the hybrid tea rose.

• **Tea rose** This dainty rose, which smells like tea leaves, was introduced from China about 1808.

• **Noisette** This was the first hybrid rose group to originate in North America—in Charleston, South Carolina.

Modern Roses

In 1867 the American Rose Society presented its first hybrid tea rose, "La France." All roses introduced after this date are considered Modern Roses. Bred for high performance, they have an upright, elegant growing habit and

OPPOSITE, NEAR RIGHT: Old Roses The Fairy and Golden Wings in yellow.
OPPOSITE, FAR RIGHT: Hybrid roses Anna and Minuette.

an incredible color range. These are the roses you see most often in nurseries and garden centers. They are:

🌿 **Hybrid Tea** This is the most widely grown rose in the world today. Long-stemmed and brightly colored, it blooms prolifically.

🌿 **Polyantha** The name of this low-growing rose derives from the Greek word meaning multi-flowered; it produces great quantities of clustered blossoms.

🌿 **Floribunda** A result of a cross between hybrid teas and polyanthas, this rose features continual bloom and good color.

🌿 **Grandiflora** This rose, the youngest member of the group, offers dramatic colors and elegant flowers on long stems.

In 1969 the English Rose was introduced by the now renowned rose breeder David Austin. He crossed the old garden rose with the modern rose. The result combines the lush beauty of old-style roses with a repeat blooming habit and an intense fragrance, providing the best of both worlds.

OPPOSITE: This velvet bloom by Giorgio Armani is proof that roses look good no matter what they are made of!
ABOVE: Some buttons are tiny works of art, especially this one, enameled with a rose in the center.

Roses also fall into distinct garden forms:

🌿 **Shrub roses and Rugosas** These roses include bushy types that don't fit into any other group of modern roses. They are used as ground covers, bushes or hedges.

🌿 **Tree roses** Almost any modern or miniature rose can be made into a tree rose, or "standard rose." They look like topiaries and need careful pruning.

🌿 **Miniature roses** These small plants, discovered in a Swiss village in 1916, grow no higher than about two feet, making them ideal for containers and window boxes.

🌿 **Climbing roses** These roses grow on long, rigid canes; they do not climb on their own but need to be trained and secured over arbors and trellises.

🌿 **Rambling roses** These roses bloom in clusters on slender, flexible canes. They will grow with abandon up the trunks of trees and gracefully wrap around pillars with a bit of help.

If you'd like to know more about what roses to plant or about their history, I have included a list of some of my favorite books, which I think you'll enjoy, on page 139.

GATHER YE

ROSEBUDS

In the garden, after a rainfall, you can faintly, yes, hear the breaking of new blooms.

Truman Capote

SELECTING 2

Years ago, French writer Alphonse Karr said, "Some people are always grumbling because roses have thorns; I am thankful that thorns have roses." This chapter is about what to do with the roses and the thorns!

We all want our roses to last as long as possible, whether we receive them as a gift or are fortunate enough to have a rose garden and have hundreds of blooms to choose from. They should look as gloriously fresh indoors as they do in the garden. All this takes is a little work!

Here are some easy tips to help you select healthy roses, along with instructions on what to do to them to make them last as long as possible—and as beautifully as possible.

27

Tips for Buying Roses

I always suggest to people that they buy their flowers from a reliable florist, using the same one regularly if they can. As a rule, florists stock the healthiest and best specimens, and they condition the flowers properly so that they last as long as possible.

If you buy your flowers anywhere else, examine them carefully. If they don't look fresh there, they will look worse when you get them home. Here are some guidelines for choosing the freshest roses:

- Flower heads should look perky, not droopy. The petals should not be bruised or crushed. Look for buds at different stages of opening for a more interesting flower arrangement.
- The leaves on the stems should be green and healthy, not wilted or discolored. As I said in my book *Simply Flowers,* healthy foliage indicates a healthy flower.
- The stems should be straight and strong. If the ends are spongy or discolored, don't buy the roses.
- When you are bringing your flowers home, it's important to make sure they are protected from heat and cold. Make your visit to the florist the last stop of the day, and bring the flowers inside as soon as possible.

Gathering Roses from the Garden

If you have a rose garden, you'll want to bring indoors some of the lush beauty and fragrance that the roses display outside. Here are some suggestions for picking them:

- Always gather your roses in early morning, when their scent is strongest and when they are able to retain the greatest amount of moisture.
- Cut the stems cleanly on a slant, using sharp florist's shears or a knife. Never use scissors as they pinch the stems closed.
- Set a water-filled bucket in a shady spot in the garden. As soon as you cut your flowers, place them *immediately* in the water. Avoid overcrowding and crushing.
- Choose roses without blemishes and in various stages of opening, including buds. The flower heads should feel firm and crisp. Stems should be strong.
- I always cut extra foliage from my rose bushes so I can have more options when I'm arranging them.

PREVIOUS PAGE: I used these trusty old rose clippers to cut an Apothecary rose from the garden.

ABOVE: A pin-prick picture of a flower-filled basket, circa 1860.

OPPOSITE, CLOCKWISE: The back room of a favorite florist, where flowers sit waiting to be arranged; in June, roses fill an old rose basket set on the stone steps leading to our cutting garden; and the trellis entrance to my garden.

HOUSE and GARDEN

June, 1938

A Condé Nast Publication

Garden Furnishings
Price 35 Cents

Conditioning Your Roses

Whether you purchase your roses from a florist, receive them as a gift or pick them in your garden, they must be prepared *before* you put them in a vase. Many people do not do this, and that's why they complain that their flowers do not last long enough. Remember that by cutting the flower from its plant, you have removed it from its source of sustenance: water. How you prepare your roses, before you arrange them in a vase, will determine how they will look and how long they will last.

The moment you bring your roses into the house, put them in a deep container of water. I use tall metal florist's pails and fill them almost to the top with tepid or warm water, which the stems absorb more quickly than cold. Then I put the container in a cool spot in my garage for at least several hours, if not overnight, so the roses can take a nice long drink.

When you are ready to arrange the flowers, you must remove the foliage that will be below the water line, because any leaves that are left in water will rot, shortening the life of your roses and fouling the water in the vase. This is also a good time to carefully remove the thorns. You can use a razor or a sharp knife for this task. The foliage on the upper part of the stems can be left, which will give the rose a more natural look, or you can remove the leaves totally, saving the pretty ones to use later in the arrangement.

Then you must cut the tips of the stems again, this time *under water*. This will prevent air bubbles from flowing up the stem and blocking the flow of water, thus shortening the life of the rose. You can do this in two ways:

1. Fill a sink full with tepid water and holding each stem under the water, cut off half an inch on a slant with sharp florist's shears.

OPPOSITE: We duplicated the cover of this 1930s magazine using one of my old English garden trugs.

ABOVE: The tools I use most often are (top to bottom) sharp pruners; special clippers that hold the thorny stems until released; and garden shears for arranging roses.

2. Use an underwater stem cutter. Fill it with water and screw on the top, which has a cutting mechanism built in. When you push the rose into it, the tip of the stem is automatically cut on a slant under water. (See Source Guide.) Now you're ready to start arranging!

Reviving Roses

Roses can usually be refreshed by one of several easy methods, so try these before you do anything rash!

- If your roses look tired, an easy way to refresh them is to mist the flowers and their leaves with cool water.
- If the rose heads are droopy, take a straight pin and prick the stem directly under the base of the head. This will release the trapped air bubble and allow the rose to absorb water.
- To perk up a bouquet of roses, give them a bath. Immerse the bouquet for fifteen minutes in a bathtub filled with cool water. The entire flower (including leaves and blooms) will soak up as much water as possible.
- If your bouquet becomes limp, recut the ends of the stems, roll the roses in a cone of newspaper, stand them in a bucket filled with cold water up to their necks and leave them overnight.
- If your roses are wilting, recut the ends of the stems and place them in several inches of hot water. Let them sit for a few minutes until they revive, and then place them in a vase filled with cold water. This also eliminates air bubbles in the stems.

ABOVE: Always cut the tips of your roses again before arranging them in a vase. This underwater stem cutter makes the job easier to do. OPPOSITE: One of the several ways to revive very wilted roses is to give them a bath! Here, I've filled a tub with cold water.

God has given us

our memories that

we might have

roses

in December.

J.M. Barrie

3 DRYING

I started drying flowers the day I got my first wrist corsage. I continued drying them in my shop, Cherchez. Then I wrote a book called *The Scented Room*. I'm happy to say that after many years, the book is still going strong and more people than ever are recycling their flowers!

The fact is, you can have a rose-filled home all winter long if you plan ahead. Every time someone sends me flowers, I dry them. All spring and summer, I harvest every rose and petal that I can from the garden. As I said in *The Scented Room,* "Why shouldn't we recycle the beauty that is growing around us outside into lovely fragrant things for use indoors?" It's easy, especially with roses. Here's how to keep your home filled with flowers all year long.

Hang-Drying

Hang-drying is the easiest way to dry roses, especially if you are drying large quantities. You simply tie together large bunches of flowers and suspend them, upside down, to dry. You can hang the bunches on hooks or nails along a beam, on old laundry and quilt racks or even on a clothesline hung in an attic. You can increase the number of flowers you can dry by suspending your bunches from hangers and then hanging those on the clothesline or hook. Be sure to choose a place that is dry and not too bright (so the flowers won't fade)—an attic, garage or even a roomy closet will work well. Here's how:

🌢 Gather your roses, leaving the longest stems possible. Strip off all the leaves.

🌢 Use about five stems per bunch, depending on how full the roses are. I sometimes hang each rose separately because they dry more perfectly that way.

🌢 Bunch your roses together with rubber bands. The stems of your bouquet will shrink as it dries, and the rubber bands will adjust down to size. You can easily loop the rubber band in order to hang the bunches quickly.

🌢 Leave space around each bunch when hanging them so the air can circulate. Remember that larger bunches will take longer to dry than smaller ones. Individual stems should not be tangled, as they have a tendency to break off when dried.

🌢 The drying time can take from several days to a week. Correctly dried roses should be as crisp as cornflakes. Any flower heads or petals that fall off can be used in potpourri or sachets.

PREVIOUS PAGE: An antique leather case holds cards with flowers engraved on them. These floral conversation cards were popular in the Victorian era.

BELOW: There are usually roses like these hanging on the drying racks in our garage and potting shed.

OPPOSITE: I like to use old wire biscuit trays for drying. The one on top has rose heads in various states of dryness. The one below holds fresh rose petals.

OPPOSITE: Roses nestled in a box of silica gel, ready to be covered with another layer of the powder. This method ensures vivid color and good shape retention.

ABOVE: Dried roses stored in a stiff paper box.

Air-Drying

This method is an easy way to dry rose heads and loose rose petals. All you need is a flat surface that allows the air to circulate around it. I like to use my collection of old wire biscuit cooling racks but you can also use small window screens, flat baskets or even newspapers laid flat on the floor or workbench. Here's how:

🌹 Place rose heads in a single layer in rows, facing up.

🌹 Spread petals in a single layer on a flat surface.

🌹 When the roses crackle like cornflakes, they are fully dried. This will take anywhere from several days to a week.

Silica Gel

Silica gel is a powdery sandlike substance that absorbs moisture; this makes it perfect for drying flowers, especially roses. If done properly, your roses will look almost as if they were fresh, retaining their original shape and color. Silica gel can be purchased at craft stores and in good nurseries. Roses dried this way can be placed on top of potpourri for decoration or used in wreaths, bouquets and flower arrangements. It's easy to use:

1. Fill a container, such as a plastic shoe or sweater box, one-third full with silica gel.

2. Choosing perfect roses, arrange the flowers face up, nestling them into the mixture.

3. Using a tablespoon, gently cover the entire blossom with the silica powder. In order to retain the original shape of the rose, you must be sure to sprinkle silica in between the petals.

4. Cover the box and leave it for several days.

5. The rose heads are ready when they are dry but not too brittle. Carefully remove each with a slotted spoon.

6. If any powder remains on the rose, gently brush it off with a soft paintbrush. If desired, you can easily reglue any petals that fall off with clear household glue.

Other Drying Methods

There are several other methods for drying roses. One is freeze-drying, which is very expensive as it requires special freezers. This is the method that is used commercially. Roses dried this way retain their original shape

and intensity of color. At the present time it is not possible to freeze-dry roses at home, but you can buy them (see "Source Guide").

You can also use your oven or microwave to dry roses. However, I prefer the basic method of air-drying, because it requires less supervision.

Storing

The way you store your dried roses is very important because you don't want all your hard work to go to waste. It's easy—just choose a place that is dry (dampness invites mold to form on the roses) and dark (the colors will fade if left in bright light). If you live in a house, an ideal storage area is the attic or garage. Apartment dwellers can use a walk-in closet, kitchen shelf or even the space under a bed.

I like to store my dried roses in heavy cardboard or plastic shoeboxes with tight tops. I line the boxes with paper towels or cotton batting, and store the roses in rows separated by tissue paper. As extra insurance I shake a little silica gel into each box to guard against dampness.

LEFT: A rosebud delicately embroidered in silk threads.
OPPOSITE: These fragile freeze-dried roses will keep their shape because they arrived neatly packed.

They that
have ros

Never
need bread.

Dorothy Parker

THE ROSE 4 PANTRY

One of the unexpected pleasures of roses is that they can be used in the kitchen in special and satisfying ways.

There is nothing nicer on a cold December morning than sweetening a steaming mug of tea with some rose-scented honey—it really does prolong the beauty of summer in the nicest way.

These recipes also make thoughtful presents when you want to bring a homemade gift to a friend. Just use an attractive container, add pretty ribbons and a label, and you have a gift that comes from the heart.

Do remember that the roses you use in cooking must be from fragrant bushes that are free from disease and pesticides. You must wash and dry them thoroughly before you use them, nevertheless.

Rose-Petal Vinegar

I've been making herbal vinegars ever since I wrote The Scented Room, *but I never made rose vinegars until recently. You can use cider or red or white wine vinegar as a base. The rose flavor adds zest to salads and desserts containing fruits. I've included two versions here and each yields one quart.*

How-To

1. Rinse and gently dry the rose petals.

2. Pour the vinegar into a saucepan and heat to the boiling point. Remove immediately from the heat.

3. Place the rose petals in a mixing bowl and pour the hot vinegar over them. Let cool.

4. Pour the mixture into the wine bottles, cork and let sit for a day or two.

5. Strain out the petals and refill the bottles.

Old-Fashioned Version

1. Rinse and gently dry the rose petals.

2. Put some rose petals into each wine bottle, pour in the vinegar and cork.

3. Put in a sunny place and leave for 2 weeks, shaking each bottle gently every other day.

4. Strain out the rose petals and refill the bottles.

Ingredients

1 cup fresh
   fragrant rose
   petals*
4 cups vinegar
Clean empty
   wine bottles
Clean corks

Remember to use pesticide-free rose petals.

PAGE 45: The rose Bluebird on an antique silver dessert fork.

OPPOSITE: Decorate your simple vinegar bottles using artificial rose leaves, string or ribbon and your own creativity.
ABOVE: An eighteenth-century bag embroidered with silk and metallic threads.

Scented Rose Sugar

Every time I serve scented sugars, my guests are delighted with this unexpected touch. In addition to fresh rose petals you can scent sugar with rose geranium leaves, orange peel, lemon slices and even vanilla beans. Scented sugar is delicious sprinkled on cookies or simple pound cakes, or used to sweeten desserts and drinks, especially iced teas. These aromatic sugars also make unusual hostess gifts when packaged prettily in tins.

Ingredients

Fresh fragrant
  rose petals*
Granulated
  sugar
Mason jars

Remember to use pesticide-free rose petals.

ABOVE: A glass plaque found in a Paris flea market.
OPPOSITE: Mason jars of granulated sugars scented with rose petals and rose geranium leaves.
BELOW: One of my cake dishes, painted with roses and forget-me-nots.

How-To

1. Rinse the rose petals and dry them thoroughly.

2. Alternate the layers of rose petals and sugar until the jar is completely filled, and seal tightly.

3. Set aside and let the rose scent infuse the sugar for several days.

4. Discard the rose petals by picking them out or by straining the sugar through a colander.

5. Then pour the sugar into fresh jars and store in a cool place.

Jasmine Rose Tea

I don't think there is anything more soothing or civilizing than a cup of hot tea. And judging by all the wonderful new herbal and floral teas now available, most of you must agree! This recipe is especially nice because it is lightly fragrant as well as comforting. Just make sure you use the most fragrant rose petals possible.

To make a perfect cup of tea, be sure to prewarm your teapot. It really does make a difference in the quality of the brew.

How-To

1. Rinse the rose petals and geranium leaves. Pat dry.

2. With scissors, cut off the bitter-tasting white base from each rose petal.

3. Warm the teapot by pouring in some hot water and swirling it about. Then discard the water.

4. Place the tea, petals and leaves in the warmed teapot.

5. Fill with the boiling water and let steep for 5 to 7 minutes.

6. When serving, sweeten the tea with rose-flavored honey or sugar (pages 55 and 48).

Yield: 2 cups of tea

Ingredients

¼ cup fresh fragrant rose petals*
4 rose geranium leaves*
2 teaspoons jasmine tea
2 cups boiling water

Remember to use pesticide-free rose petals and geranium leaves.

OPPOSITE: I enjoy buying old teacups and saucers. They're all different but coordinate because they have floral themes.

Rose Geranium Cake

Almost everyone likes pound cake, and here's one with a little something different. It features the scented geranium, a wonderful plant that comes in a great variety of fragrances including lemon, cinnamon, apple and, my favorite, rose. It looks charming growing in the garden and does double duty as a wonderful accent in the kitchen. You can top this cake with a raspberry puree and either whipped cream or softened vanilla ice cream for a delicious four-star dessert.

Ingredients

15 fresh rose
    geranium
    leaves*
Loaf baking pan
Parchment
    paper
Your favorite
    pound cake
    recipe or
    packaged mix

*Remember to use
pesticide-free rose
geranium leaves.*

ABOVE: I love using geranium leaves in my flower arranging and my cooking! OPPOSITE: Fresh rose geranium leaves from the garden on this simple, tasty pound cake.

How-To

1. Rinse and thoroughly dry the rose geranium leaves.

2. Spray the baking pan with nonstick spray and line the sides and bottom with parchment paper.

3. Arrange the leaves on the sides and bottom of the loaf pan, pressing to flatten them against the paper.

4. Trying not to disturb the leaves, carefully pour the pound cake batter into the pan. Bake as directed.

5. After the cake has cooled, remove it from the pan.

6. Set on a serving dish, and decorate with additional rose geranium leaves if desired.

Yield: 1 loaf cake

Rose-Flavored Honey

I'm a real honey fan and love going to farms in our area to buy the freshest honey available. With this recipe I'm able to take local honey and give it a personal touch by adding rose petals from my garden. Even though it may seem old-fashioned, our nieces and nephews enjoy receiving this sweet, healthy gift in care packages when they are away at school. You can also use herbs, such as thyme, basil or mint, and other flowers—lavender, for example—to flavor honey in attractive and tasty ways.

How-To

1. Rinse and gently dry the rose petals.

2. With scissors, cut off the bitter-tasting white base from each petal.

3. Chop the rose petals into small pieces on a cutting board.

4. Pour the honey into a saucepan and heat it over a low flame for a minute or two until softened.

5. Remove the honey from the heat, and stir in the rose petals. Let cool.

6. Pour into the glass jar.

Yield: 1 pint of honey

Ingredients

½ cup fresh
   fragrant rose
   petals*
2 cups honey
Glass jar

Remember to use pesticide-free rose petals.

OPPOSITE: Sweet rose honey ready for the breakfast table.
LEFT: Delicate apricot roses in a cream jug.

And **I will**

make thee

beds of

roses

and a thousand fragrant posies.

Christopher Marlowe

LOTIONS AND POTIONS

Since ancient times, roses have been used to enhance and comfort the body. In fact, Elizabeth I was presented each January with snowballs scented with fragrant rosewater.

The current revival of old-fashioned recipes has made all of us much more aware of how flowers and plants can affect our feeling of well-being. Included here are some refreshing and inspiring ideas using roses that will lift your spirits as well as your body. They make thoughtful gifts, especially for friends who are always on the go and would enjoy a soothing surprise.

Rose-Petal Splash and Fabric Wash

We consider rose water to be so romantic because it was first made hundreds of years ago in Persia, where the most luscious roses grew. Today you can buy rose water. But why bother when it's so easy to make?

Every June after my roses have bloomed, I make a batch and keep it refrigerated in glass jars. Before houseguests arrive, I pour the water into pretty bottles for them to use as a cooling and refreshing face splash.

It's nice, too, used in finger bowls at the table. You can also throw a cup of this rose water into the final rinse cycle to gently scent your bath towels. Spritz your sheets and pillowcases with it before ironing, to ensure sweet dreams.

Ingredients

1 cup fresh fragrant rose petals
3 cups distilled water
4 drops rose essential oil
Glass bottles or jars

How-To

1. Rinse the rose petals.

2. Drain and then put them in a bowl.

3. Boil the distilled water and pour it over the rose petals. Leave for several hours to steep.

4. Strain out the rose petals and stir in the rose essential oil.

5. Store in tightly closed jars in the refrigerator.

Yield: 1½ pints

PREVIOUS PAGE: This is the charming frontispiece from a rare little book entitled *The Lady's Toilet*, dated 1888.

THIS PAGE: A favorite souvenir of Italy—rose water from Florence.
OPPOSITE: A bottle of homemade rose water made from the fragrant Salet roses that grow in our garden.

Relaxing Foot Bath

This is a wonderful recipe to make if you have an herb garden because you can use a variety of botanicals, depending on what is in bloom. There's nothing nicer than unwinding at the end of a strenuous day by soaking tired, aching feet for five or ten minutes in this soothing concoction.

How-To

1. Pour the water into a saucepan and add the rose petals, bay leaves and sprigs of herbs.

2. Bring the mixture to a boil and simmer for 5 minutes. Let cool.

3. Strain out the petals and herbs, and pour the liquid into jars. Then stir in the brandy. Tightly cap, and store in the refrigerator. (It should last about 2 weeks.)

4. Add 1 cup of the mixture to a footbath or bucket filled with tap water.

5. If desired, add Epsom salts, which soothes sore muscles.

Yield: 2 quarts

Ingredients

8 cups water
1 cup fresh
　fragrant
　rose petals
2 bay leaves
20 sprigs of any
　combination
　of lavender,
　lemon balm,
　lemon verbena,
　marjoram,
　rosemary
　and thyme
Glass jars
1 teaspoon
　brandy

OPPOSITE: This Victorian washbowl is ideal for a foot bath, with some fresh lemon balm and rose petals thrown in for extra fragrance.
THIS PAGE: A colorful antique saucer with some fresh-picked treasures.

Fragrant Talcum Powder

When I was a child, there was a large round box of talcum powder on my mother's dressing table. It had a big fluffy puff and symbolized everything I thought about what it was to be "grown-up." In addition to the luxury of powdering up after a bath, this scented talc can be used in place of potpourri to fill sachets.

Ingredients

8 oz unscented
talcum
powder
15 drops rose
water
Glass jars

How-To

1. Put the talcum powder in a mixing bowl.

2. Add the rose water and gently stir with a spoon. If the fragrance is not strong enough, add more rose water. Try not to get the mixture too wet.

3. Let sit for approximately 1 hour or until the powder feels dry.

4. Place in decorative covered jars with large openings.

Yield: 8 ounces of scented talcum

RIGHT: A delicate, old box, circa 1820, which once held precious cologne.
OPPOSITE: Treat yourself to an antique silver vanity jar for your talcum powder. Perhaps it will come, like this one, with a fluffy puff in it!

Aromatherapy Oils

Although I think the benefits of aromatherapy can be exaggerated, when I'm in the doldrums, it does lift my spirits to dab some fragrant oil on my wrists. Put a drop on a pumice stone or seashell, which will absorb the fragrance, too.

Here are two potions I couldn't live without—one is for refreshing, perfect for after a long trip; the other is for relaxing, especially nice after work. The directions are the same, only the ingredients vary slightly.

You can use either grapeseed oil or almond oil (almond oil has a definite fragrance). Both can be purchased at supermarkets and health food stores.

How-To

1. Pour all the oils into the bottle and close tightly.

2. Shake the bottle several times to combine the oils.

3. Transfer to a decorative bottle if desired.

Yield: 1 ounce of fragrant oil

Relaxing Oil Ingredients

4 tablespoons grapeseed oil
5 drops rose essential oil
3 drops lavender essential oil
1-ounce glass bottle

Refreshing Oil Ingredients

4 tablespoons grapeseed oil
5 drops rose or rose geranium essential oil
3 drops peppermint essential oil
1-ounce glass bottle

OPPOSITE: It's fun to put your fragrant oils into elegant bottles like this one of cut glass from the 1940s.

Rose Cuticle Cream

The simple pleasures of life, like giving myself a manicure, always make me feel better. As a finishing touch, soak your hands in a bowl of warm water and lemon juice, dry off and apply this rich cream to your cuticles. Leave it on for about five minutes and then wipe it off. Now, you're ready for polish.

The ingredients are easy to find—almond oil at the supermarket, lanolin and cocoa butter in the drugstore, and beeswax at a craft store (see "Source Guide"). Be sure to use an old double boiler as the pot can be difficult to get clean.

Ingredients

4 tablespoons almond oil

1½ tablespoons beeswax

1½ tablespoons cocoa butter

1 tablespoon lanolin

8 drops rose essential oil

2 small covered plastic jars

How-To

1. Pour the almond oil into the top of a double boiler. Then add the beeswax, cocoa butter and lanolin.

2. Warm over low heat until all the ingredients have melted.

3. Working quickly, remove from the heat, add the essential oil and stir.

4. Immediately pour the mixture into small plastic jars.

5. Do not use until the mixture has cooled.

Yield: 2 small jars of cuticle cream

THIS PAGE AND OPPOSITE: These delicate brass hands were used as paper clips in the Victorian era in England.

Rose-Scented Ink

It's fun to scent notepaper by tucking a small rose sachet (see page 88) into your stationery box. The paper, which is porous, absorbs the aroma and makes writing a letter more enjoyable! You can take this idea a step further by making your own scented ink. It is simple, but do remember to make sure your work surface is ink-stain-proof. I also suggest using a dark-color ink, as the vodka and the oil will dilute it.

How-To

1. Pour the ink into the decorative bottle, using the glass funnel. (A glass funnel can be washed out; a plastic one will retain the ink stains.)

2. Mix the vodka and essential oil together in a glass measuring cup. (The vodka helps the ink and oil blend properly.)

3. Slowly add this mixture to the ink.

4. Screw the top on tightly and *gently* shake.

Yield: 1 bottle of scented ink

Ingredients

Bottle of red, blue or black ink (1 ounce)
Small decorative bottle
Small glass funnel
20 drops unscented vodka
4 drops rose essential oil

OPPOSITE: Take a break from your computer and write a letter to a good friend using scented inks you've made yourself. THIS PAGE: I found these old postcards, circa 1900, at a flea market in the South of France.

A ROSE

IS BEST

a flowerless room is a soulless room.

Vita Sackville-West

ARRANGING

"A rose was one of the few flowers, he said, that looked better picked than growing. A bowl of roses in a drawing-room had a depth of colour and scent they had not possessed in the open.... In the house they became mysterious and subtle." Maxim de Winter, the pensive hero in *Rebecca,* has a point. Roses *are* wonderful in the garden, but when they are gathered together inside, they are extraordinary. We're drawn to their sumptuousness and can't help but lean over to catch their scent—they focus our attention. At the Manderley of *Rebecca,* there were roses in the house for eight months of the year—would that we were all so fortunate!

This chapter is about treasuring the roses you *do* have and savoring their beauty at home. There are so many luscious ways to decorate with them; I hope you discover some you like as you turn these pages.

My approach to flower arranging has not changed since I wrote about it in *Simply Flowers*. I do consider it a form of creative self-expression, but I think that if we take it too seriously, the fun disappears—and the finished flower arrangement is joyless as well. There are no rules here, only guidelines. Try to enjoy yourself and the roses. Don't fuss too much—an overdone bouquet lacks naturalness and spontaneity.

The good news is that roses are easy to arrange, so experiment with them. They look elegant left on their slender stems in a small vase or cut short and arranged in low mounds. Sometimes, when I'm feeling adventurous, I like cutting the stems off entirely and floating the rose blossoms in bowls to be used as a centerpiece or as finger bowls at the table.

Most of us have been given a dozen roses at one time or another, and so I've included a few ideas for arranging them. The first thing you must decide is what length you want the stems to be. Many people are hesitant about trimming the long stems of their roses. The length of the stems gives you flexibility, but it should not intimidate you! If rose stems are left too long, your arrangement can look meager and spindly. Shortening the stems

PREVIOUS SPREAD, LEFT: An untidy bouquet of roses, including the fringe-petaled Grooten-dorst in a cobalt glass vase. PREVIOUS SPREAD, RIGHT: A boutonniere of Fairy roses.

BELOW: Vivid red roses skim the surface in this glass bowl, which is cleverly lit from underneath.
OPPOSITE: Deep pink blossoms float in Chinese porcelain finger bowls ready to be placed on the table. With enough of them, you don't need a centerpiece.

can make a dramatic difference, high-lighting the shape of each flower head. Remember, too, that roses are usually priced according to stem length, so if you are purchasing your own, you can save money by planning ahead and buying only the length you're going to use.

When arranging your roses, make sure that they are not all facing in the same direction. They should also stand at different heights to give a feeling of depth. Look at how the flowers grow in nature. Your composition should look as artless as possible.

It's fun to mix roses with other flow-ers, and this makes for a more rustic bouquet. Some of my favorite combi-nations include a range of pink roses with full-blown peonies, from pale blush to dark fuchsia; pink or red roses with lush lilacs or French lavender (the purple complements deep red roses or apricot roses gloriously); and roses with viburnum or lady's mantle (the chartreuse green is a great foil for roses of almost any color). Consider your own color preferences. But if you're just starting out, remember it's always easier to arrange flowers in the

Various ways to arrange a dozen roses. CLOCKWISE, FROM ABOVE LEFT: White roses look elegant in glass vases; pale Heritage roses in a pottery vase; long-stemmed roses with hydrangeas and ferns; small bouquets featur-ing, left to right, Queen Anne's lace, ferns and lamb's ears; grape leaves and apricot roses with their stems cut very short.

same color family than to create a complex multicolor bouquet.

Don't forget to incorporate texture into your composition. For example, include leaves like lamb's ears, which have a matte feel, or the pale artemisias for their delicate gray texture; light green ferns, which are smooth and graceful; or even the shiny rose leaves themselves, some of which should be saved when you are conditioning them. I especially like to use rose geranium leaves, which add scent as well as beauty.

Fruits and vegetables also add texture and unexpected interest. Don't forget to incorporate rose hips, if you have them growing in your garden, for their richness of color in the fall.

Making Roses Last Longer

Don't neglect your flowers after you have arranged them. Your roses will last longer if you:

&. Top off the vases daily with lukewarm water. You don't have to remove the flowers. If you can, put the vase in the sink and flush out the old water with the new.

It's fun to mix roses with other flowers and leaves. CLOCKWISE, FROM OPPOSITE TOP: Peonies mixed with Gertrude Jekyll roses; apricot roses with green viburnum; Gertrude Jekyll roses with purple irises; Graham Thomas with flowering lady's mantle; various roses with lady's mantle; fragrant Ballerina roses with daisies.

🌹 Mist your roses, as blossoms and leaves both absorb moisture.

🌹 Never place a vase of roses in direct sun or in a cold draft.

🌹 Add one of the following to the vase water:

- the packet of commercial flower food supplied by the florist—it works
- naturally absorbent charcoal or several drops of household bleach to neutralize stagnant odors
- an aspirin to limit the loss of moisture to the air
- a little sugar or lemonade to help move moisture through the stems

🌹 Always rinse containers out with household bleach to help remove bacteria, and dry them thoroughly after use.

Use vegetables with roses for unique results.
OPPOSITE, CLOCKWISE: Asparagus and artichokes; yellow pattypan squash and eggplants; zucchini and artichokes; Oriental eggplants.
ABOVE LEFT: This antique Wedgwood rose bowl has holes in the top in which to place the stems.
ABOVE RIGHT: White Rose of York looking elegant.

Containers

Just a word about containers: It's hard for roses to look bad in just about anything you put them in—from glass to silver to the many varieties of ceramic vases, antique porcelain cache-pots, terra-cotta pots and woven baskets available. Just make sure that the container you choose is in harmony with the tones of the roses that you expect to use.

Have fun at antiques shows looking for unexpected containers, like the "slop bowls" from old tea sets that were originally used to hold the used tea leaves. Their shape and depth make them perfect for old roses.

I love using my small collection of antique rose bowls—really pots with pierced lids, which were made so the roses could just be plunked into the holes. Using them, the harried Victorian housewife could get creative with a minimum of fuss or skill. (Things haven't changed all that much!)

And some of my favorite containers came from tag sales, including old pitchers, which, with their narrow

necks, make beautiful flower arranging an easy task. I also enjoy small flower holders like salt cellars, old cordial glasses and christening cups. These are just right for holding, as Dorothy Parker's poem says, "One Perfect Rose" for individual table settings and guest rooms.

ABOVE, LEFT: Roses from the garden set in silver cups. RIGHT: Rose heads and petunias look perfect at each place setting.
BELOW, LEFT: Yellow roses tucked into one of my favorite little jugs handmade in Austria.
RIGHT: A cut-glass salt cellar arranged with various blossoms.
OPPOSITE: A single rose always looks good. Here, Golden Wings and New Dawn are set in hand-blown bud vases.

Perfume

is

what

the

flowers

throw

away.

Paul Valéry

POTPOURRI
AND SACHETS

When I wrote *The Scented Room* I had no idea it would become such a classic. It covers everything you need to know about making potpourri and sachets, so in this chapter I'll simply give you the "rose" version of each, focusing on my favorite recipes made with dried rosebuds, petals and fragrant oils.

I still believe that smell is the most underrated of all the senses, and I agree with the philosopher Jean-Jacques Rousseau, who said, "Smell is the sense of the imagination."

I love to decorate with potpourri because I know that when people walk into my home, they are welcomed not only by its luscious fragrance but by its soothing comfort as well. We have all experienced the calming influence created by a beautiful scent, and roses are the best source of this.

85

Spicy Rose Potpourri

Ingredients

1 oz powdered
  orris root
1 oz powdered
  cinnamon
1 oz powdered
  allspice
1 oz powdered
  cloves
2 oz lavender
  flowers
2 oz whole
  cloves
1 oz cinnamon
  sticks
5 drops
  lavender
  essential oil
20 drops rose
  essential oil
3 oz rose petals
4 oz rosebuds

The rich scent of this potpourri comes from the combination of dried roses with lavender and spices. I like to fill a bowl almost to the top with a potpourri and then finish it off with rose heads that I have dried all summer.

Remember to refresh your potpourri whenever you feel the fragrance has faded. Fill an eyedropper with the best rose essential oil you can buy, and insert it under the rose heads, so the oil is absorbed by the potpourri. Store your oils in glass bottles in a cool, dark spot.

How-To

1. Mix the powdered spices and lavender flowers together in a large pottery or glass bowl.

2. Add the whole cloves and cinnamon sticks and stir.

3. Using an eyedropper, scatter the lavender and rose oils over the mixture. Stir again.

4. Carefully add the dried rose petals and buds, stirring gently to avoid crushing them.

5. Place the mixture in a brown paper bag that is lined with wax paper, and store in a dry, cool place to cure for about 2 weeks.

6. After it's cured, the potpourri is ready to be placed in a decorative container. Add extra rose heads if desired.

Yield: 1 pound of potpourri

PREVIOUS PAGE: It's easy to make a sachet like this. Fold a wide piece of ribbon in half, sew up both sides, then fill it with your favorite recipe.

RIGHT: A Victorian needlepoint belt. OPPOSITE: The roses I dried last summer, set atop a bowl of potpourri.

Rose Sachets

A sachet is really just potpourri in a bag. It can be tucked just about anywhere you want fragrance to linger—closets, armoires, blanket chests and drawers. In The Scented Room *I even owned up to carrying a sachet in my handbag! Here are two recipes I especially like. The directions are the same for both, only the ingredients change.*

One, Rose Moth Bags, will help deter moths and pleasantly scent your storage spaces. The other, Geranium Sweet Bag, has a special, subtle fragrance.

How-To

1. In a pottery bowl, combine all the dry ingredients and stir.

2. Using an eyedropper, add the essential oil(s) to the mixture and blend.

3. Place the mixture in a brown paper bag that is lined with wax paper, and store in a dry, cool place to cure for about 2 weeks.

Yield for each blend: 1 pound, or enough to fill about 1 dozen small bags

Rose Moth Bag Ingredients

3 oz whole cloves
1 oz powdered orris root
3 oz lavender flowers
3 oz cedar shavings
3 oz cut vetiver
3 oz rose petals
20 drops rose essential oil

Geranium Sweet Bag Ingredients

8 oz rose petals
6 oz rose geranium leaves
2 oz powdered orris root
10 drops rose essential oil
10 drops rose geranium essential oil

OPPOSITE: Little muslin bags are just perfect for filling with any potpourri.
LEFT: A selection of organdy sachets from France.

Honor women! They wreathe... heavenly roses into earthly life.

Johann von Schiller

SILK AND DRIED DECORATIONS

Most of us love roses so much that it doesn't matter if they are fresh, dried, silk, beaded, porcelain or even paper—we like having them around in any form! In the film version of Fannie Flagg's book *Fried Green Tomatoes at the Whistle Stop Cafe,* Jessica Tandy points to the walls of her depressing room in a nursing home, which she has covered with pictures of flowers, and says, "Do you like my roses? Since I don't have a garden, I made me a paper garden—I've got everything but the bugs." You could say this is one of the advantages of silk and dried decorations! If you use them, buy the best quality available and don't compare them to fresh roses, because they have a charm all their own.

Dried-Rose Wreath

Ingredients

22-gauge craft
    wire
Straw wreath
    form
Botanicals with
    stems, such
    as artemisia,
    boxwood,
    heather,
    larkspur
Florist's pins
Dried flower
    heads, such
    as roses,
    peonies,
    hydrangea,
    yarrow,
    coxcomb
Glue gun

Wreaths say "welcome" in the nicest way! If they are dried, they can be used inside as well as outdoors, over fireplace mantels and in bedrooms in place of paintings. They add warmth, color and texture to a room.

To keep your wreath looking fresh, never place it in direct sunlight, avoid rooms with high humidity, and dust it every so often with a soft paintbrush.

When you buy the straw wreath form for this project, remember that when you finish the wreath, it will be two to four inches larger than the form.

How-To

1. Make a loop of wire at the top of the wreath form so you can hang it later.

2. Wire four stems of the same botanical together into a bunch, leaving 1 inch of stem below the wire. Repeat, using all the botanical sprigs.

3. Attaching them with florist's pins, layer the bunches around the front of the form, going in the same direction, until you have covered the entire front of the wreath.

4. Next, decide where you will place the flower heads on the wreath. Remember to arrange them at slightly different depths and in random directions so the wreath has a natural, graceful look to it.

5. Carefully hot-glue each flower head to the form.

PREVIOUS PAGE: I found this extraordinary, book-shaped nineteenth-century sewing case on Portobello Road in London.

OPPOSITE: To create a sumptuous wreath, use as many beautiful flowers as possible, making it look full.

Dried-Rose Basket

When properly dried, roses can last a very long time. Easy directions for drying them are in Chapter 3. In the winter months, I always make several dried rose arrangements and place them around the house as colorful touches—they really do perk up the place! This easy-to-make basket is perfect for using as a simple centerpiece when last-minute guests drop in.

How-To

1. Using the bottom of the basket as the pattern, trace the shape on a block of Sahara (the floral foam used as a basis for dried flower arrangements).

2. With a sharp florist's knife, cut the foam slightly smaller than the traced pattern.

3. Push the foam snugly into the basket, making sure it is 1 inch lower than the rim.

4. Select rose heads in a compatible color combination. Holding each rose head, cut off all but 1 inch of stem. Firmly push the stem into the foam, and continue until the entire block is covered.

5. Add moss around the edges, and tie a ribbon around the basket if desired.

Ingredients

Simple basket
Block of Sahara
  floral foam
Florist's knife
Selection of
  dried rose
  heads
Dried moss
Ribbon
  (optional)

OPPOSITE: Freeze-dried roses keep their shape and color and are perfect for using in simple arrangements like this one.

Silk flowers have been enjoyed for centuries. In *Simply Flowers* I included directions for hand-painting silk flowers; this art form was very popular in Georgian England and is now being revived. In those days, a real flower out of season was a rarity and would be forbiddingly expensive.

One of the advantages of the best-quality silk flowers is that they always look freshly picked. In fact, many people will mix silk with fresh roses for special occasions like weddings, where many flowers are needed. Though they are no substitute for the real thing, it's sometimes fun to use them: they look great on gift wrap and they don't drop petals on the carpet.

To keep them looking their best, all artificial and dried flowers should be kept away from direct sunlight, which will fade them. At that point they should be replaced. And they should also be dusted occasionally to be kept fresh-looking. You can add a small fragrant sachet or oil-scented pellet to the container if you'd like to add a subtle scent.

OPPOSITE: Boxes of French silk cabbage roses, in lovely shades of pink, ready to be packed. RIGHT: A Victorian milk-glass vase with a charming bouquet of hand-painted English blossoms arranged in it.

CELEBRATING

WITH ROSES

sweet spring,

full of

sweet days

and roses

George Herbert

ENTERTAINING

Flowers and special occasions go hand in hand. Years ago, Katherine Mansfield noted the significance of celebrating with roses in her classic story *The Garden Party*, when she said, "Roses are the only flowers that impress people at garden-parties; the only flowers that everybody is certain of knowing." Things haven't changed that much over the years. Just the other day, I read about a wedding in which hundreds of thousands of roses were used as decoration for the reception dinner.

While most of us entertain on a less lavish scale, we still most often choose roses to grace our parties. This chapter includes some clever ideas that I hope will stimulate your imagination and inspire you to use roses in new and beautiful ways.

Wedding Confetti

It's the little details that make a wedding extra-special. The sight of the new couple leaving the ceremony amidst a delicate swirl of fragrant rose petals is one everyone will remember.

Ingredients

Good-quality
  paper
Cellophane
Scotch tape
Ribbons
  (optional)
Fresh rose
  petals

PREVIOUS PAGE: This porcelain lady, with hand-painted roses strewn on her skirt, is ready for a party.

OPPOSITE: Rose-petal cones set in woven baskets. When you make one, fold the corner up at the bottom, forming the pocket which keeps the rose petals from falling out.

How-To

1. Decide how many confetti cones you will need, and cut a 6½-inch square piece of paper for each.

2. Cut an equal amount of cellophane the same size.

3. Lay the paper on a flat surface with one of the points at the bottom. Fold this bottom point up one-fifth of the way, forming a pocket.

4. Roll the paper into a cone shape and tape it together on the side.

5. Roll the cellophane around the cone, and tape it also. Add ribbon if desired.

6. Several hours before the wedding, fill each cone with about 1 cup of fresh rose petals. Arrange the cones in baskets, to be handed out to the guests when the bride and groom are about to leave.

Strawberry-Rose Sorbet

We first had these lemon cups at a party in Italy —the perfect dessert after a rich meal. They look so attractive when set on silver trays—just the thing to serve at a wedding or other celebration.

How-To

1. Wash and dry the lemons. Then cut the tops off about one-third of the way down and set them aside. Shave the bottoms so the lemons will stand up.

2. Remove the pulp from the lemon shells and tops. Recycle the pulp by adding it to lemonade or iced tea.

3. Place the lemon shells and tops in the freezer for about 3 hours.

4. Remove sorbet from the freezer and allow it to soften.

5. Hull, wash and puree the strawberries. Refrigerate the puree for 15 minutes to cool.

6. Place the softened sorbet in a large bowl. Blend in the strawberry puree and the rose water. Work quickly, because the sorbet will be melting while you mix it.

7. Remove the lemon shells from the freezer and quickly spoon the mixture into them. Then return them to the freezer for at least 1 hour, or until the sorbet is firm.

8. Before serving, place the tops on the lemons, gently pressing down. Add sprigs of herbs if desired.

Yield: 6 lemon cups

Ingredients

6 large lemons
1 pint lemon sorbet
6 strawberries
20 drops rose water
6 sprigs of lemon balm, lemon verbena or mint (optional)

OPPOSITE: A beautiful way to end a meal— serving desserts like this one that are fresh and delicious.
ABOVE: A unique ring pillow made from old laces, ribbons and silver-topped push-pins.

Rose Ice Bucket

Everyone always oohs and aahs when they see this ice bucket. Have everything lined up in advance, and enlist someone with a strong arm to help you put it in and take it out of the freezer.

Ingredients

2-gallon plastic bucket
2 gallons water, distilled
1-liter empty plastic soda bottle
Rocks
Roses on long stems
Serving tray

ABOVE: Souvenirs of places and things I've enjoyed on my travels.
OPPOSITE: A bottle of champagne cooling in a Rose Ice Bucket you can make yourself and decorate with lady's mantle.

How-To

1. Remove the shelves from your freezer so the bucket will fit in easily.

2. Fill the bucket halfway with distilled water. Cut the top off the soda bottle, and place it in the center of the water-filled bucket. Fill it with the rocks to hold it in place. (This will create the space for the bottle.)

3. Stand the roses around the outside of the soda bottle. Slowly add more distilled water until it covers the tops of the rose heads.

4. Gently place the bucket in the freezer, being careful not to dislodge the roses or unbalance the soda bottle.

5. Freeze overnight until solid. You can add more water to the top and refreeze if the roses rise to the surface.

6. To remove the soda bottle from the ice mold, take out the rocks and gently run hot water into the soda bottle. You can then lift it out.

7. To unmold, place the bucket on its side in the sink, and run hot tap water around the outside. Have your tray ready so you can immediately place the ice bucket on it.

8. Decorate the base with flowers or leaves. The bucket should stay frozen for several hours.

Rose Ice Cubes

This is an easy way to look like "the hostess with the mostest." Just adding these ice cubes to any cool drink—iced tea, lemonade or even water—will make your table look as colorful as an Impressionist painting. Small berries, such as raspberries, blueberries and fraises des bois, can be used in addition to small flowers.

How-To

1. Fill the ice cube trays one-third full with the distilled water, and place them in the freezer. (Frozen tap water can be cloudy because of the mineral content.)

2. Rinse the petals and buds. Pat dry.

3. When the ice is frozen, remove the trays from the freezer and add the petals and buds to the cubes. Then fill the trays to the top with more distilled water, and refreeze.

4. After about 30 minutes, take a peek. Push down any petals that have risen to the surface.

5. When the cubes are frozen, pop them from the trays and enjoy.

Ingredients

Ice cube trays
Distilled water
**Fresh fragrant
    rose petals
    and small
    buds***

*Remember to use pesticide-free rose petals and buds.

OPPOSITE: Multicol-ored rose and del-phinium buds make an ordinary glass of water into something very special.

Rose-Petal Plates

I've always enjoyed pressing flowers and leaves and using them in interesting ways. You can create your own china patterns by arranging fresh botanicals between two clear glass plates. In addition to rose petals you can use any delicate flat flowers like pansies, sweet peas or pinks or herb leaves like lemon verbena, mint or lady's mantle. Be sure to coordinate the colors of the petals with your table setting and the food you plan to serve.

Ingredients

Fresh colorful
rose petals
Clear dessert
or dinner
plates

How-To

1. Select large, perfect, bruise-free petals, all as close in size as possible.

2. Arrange the petals in a design on the bottom plate. Be sure to consider what you are putting on the plate, as you want the petals to show. If you prefer, this can be pre-planned on a flat surface in advance.

3. When your composition is complete, gently place the second plate on top of the first. Once it is in place, press down carefully.

ABOVE AND RIGHT: Little paper boxes covered with pressed paper and découpage. OPPOSITE: Imagine how beautiful an entire table would look set with these rose-petal plates.

Sugared Rose Petals

Roses have been used in the kitchen for centuries. In ancient Persia people buried jugs of rosebuds in their gardens; when unearthed, the roses would magically open at the table during the meal.

You can use this technique on flowers like violets, pansies, delphinium buds, nasturtium blossoms, small berries and the leaves of edible herbs. Use them to decorate desserts, especially cakes.

How-To

1. Select perfect rose petals. Gently rinse and pat them dry.

2. Beat the egg whites in one mixing bowl. Pour the sugar into another.

3. Set out a cookie sheet lined with wax paper.

4. Carefully dip each petal into the egg whites, making sure to cover both sides adequately. Then dip it into the sugar and set it on the cookie sheet.

5. When all the petals are coated, set them aside for several hours to dry.

6. Use the rose petals immediately, or store them between layers of wax paper in an airtight plastic container for up to 1 week. Do not refrigerate.

Ingredients

Fresh fragrant
rose petals*
Egg whites
Superfine sugar
Cookie sheet

*Remember to use pesticide-free rose petals.

OPPOSITE: When they are done, the sugar-coated rose petals should be set on wax paper to dry.
ABOVE: A wedding cake embellished with sweet roses and ivy vines.

EVERYTHING'S

COMING UP ROSES

Won't you come

into my

garden?

I would like

my roses

to see you.

Richard Sheridan

ROSE GARDENS
AROUND THE WORLD

I love to travel, and I think the next best thing to being there is reading about it. It's always fun finding new places and revisiting old ones.

Most of us enjoy looking at other people's gardens. Actually seeing the plant enables you to imagine it in your own garden. You can also see it up close, and of course, in the case of roses, you can smell it.

This chapter is filled with gardens that I've enjoyed visiting over the years. In addition, there are other discoveries like wonderful hotels, some of which have their own gardens and floral departments. It's the uncomplicated pleasures—like admiring a new garden on a sunny morning and having lunch afterward—that remind us of how wonderful life can be.

KISS OF THE SUN FOR PARDON
A SONG OF THE BIRDS FOR MIRTH
IS NEARER GODS HEART
IN A GARDEN
THAN ANYWHERE ELSE ON EARTH

PREVIOUS PAGE: A miniature iron figure of a gardener, circa 1920.
CLOCKWISE, ABOVE RIGHT: A garden poem amid the roses; the Orangery at Dumbarton Oaks is home to a giant creeping fig; garden statuary in the Huntington Botanical Gardens; A gate to the sumptuous roses in Old Westbury Gardens; roses bloom everywhere at Longwood Gardens.

United States of America

There are so many delightful gardens in this country that there is always one to visit or revisit, no matter where you are. Many of those listed below have stunning historic homes to explore, too.

Gardens

ALABAMA

Bellingrath Gardens
12401 Bellingrath Gardens Rd.
Theodore, AL 36582
Tel: 334-973-2217

Birmingham Botanical Garden
2612 Lane Park Dr.
Birmingham, AL 35223
Tel: 205-879-1227

ARIZONA

Reid Park Rose Garden
1100 S. Randolph Way
Tucson, AZ 85716
Tel: 520-291-4022

CALIFORNIA

Berkeley Rose Garden
1200 Euclid Ave.
Berkeley, CA 94720
Tel: 510-644-6566

Filoli
Canada Rd.
Woodside, CA 94062
Tel: 415-364-2880

Garden Valley Nursery
498 Pepper Rd.
Petaluma, CA 94952
Tel: 707-795-5266

Huntington Botanical Gardens
1151 Oxford Rd.
San Marino, CA 91108
Tel: 818-405-2100

Inez Parker Memorial Rose Garden
1549 El Prado
San Diego, CA 92101
Tel: 619-239-0512

La Mirada
720 Via Mirada
Monterey, CA 93940
Tel: 408-372-3689

Luther Burbank Home & Rose Garden
50 Mark W. Springs Rd.
Santa Rosa, CA 95403
Tel: 707-527-7006

Oakland Museum Gardens
1000 Oak St.
Oakland, CA 94607
Tel: 510-273-3401

CALIFORNIA

Bluestone Main
120 Petaluma Blvd.
Petaluma, CA 94952
Tel: 707-765-2024

A store filled with carefully chosen gifts for the garden.

Claudia Laub Stationery
7407 Beverly Blvd.
Los Angeles, CA 90036
Tel: 323-931-1710
Fax: 323-931-0126

Roses and flowers beautifully engraved on stationery and cards in this shop.

Four Seasons Aviara
7100 Four Seasons Point
Carlsbad, CA 92009
Tel: 760-603-3780
Fax: 760-603-3788

A tranquil hotel overlooking the Pacific, with its own in-house flower studio.

The French Laundry
6640 Washington St.
Yountville, CA 94599
Tel: 707-944-2380
Fax: 707-944-1944

Creative cooking at its best in this beautiful restaurant.

Hotel Bel-Air
701 Stone Canyon Rd.
Los Angeles, CA 90077
Tel: 310-472-1211
Fax: 310-476-5890

A California classic. The luxurious 12-acre garden is legendary.

Meadowood Resort Hotel
900 Meadowood Lane
St. Helena, CA 94575
Tel: 707-963-3646
Fax: 707-963-3532

A chic hideaway in the Napa Valley wine country.

The Urban Gardener
2852 East Coast Hwy.
Corona-del-Mar, CA 92625
Tel: 714-640-6972

Shop for special items for your garden here.

DISTRICT OF COLUMBIA

The Four Seasons Hotel
2800 Pennsylvania Ave., NW
Washington, DC 20007
Tel: 202-342-0444
Fax: 202-342-1673

Settle in luxuriously, have tea and explore Georgetown.

Rose Hills Memorial Park
3900 Workman Mill Rd.
Whittier, CA 90601
Tel: 301-699-0921

University of California Botanical Garden
Centennial Drive
Berkeley, CA 94720
Tel: 510-642-3343

Virginia Robinson Gardens
1008 Elden Way
Beverly Hills, CA 90210
Tel: 310-276-5367

COLORADO

Denver Botanic Garden
1005 York St.
Denver, CO 80206
Tel: 303-331-4000

CONNECTICUT

Elizabeth Park Rose Garden
150 Wallbridge
W. Hartford, CT 06119
Tel: 860-242-0017

DISTRICT OF COLUMBIA

Dumbarton Oaks
1703 32nd St., N.W.
Washington, DC 20007
Tel: 202-338-8278

ILLINOIS

Chicago Botanic Garden
1000 Lake Cook Rd.
Glencoe, IL 60022
Tel: 708-835-5440

KANSAS

Reinisch Memorial Rose Garden
4320 S.W. 10th Ave.
Topeka, KS 66604
Tel: 913-272-5900

LOUISIANA

American Rose Center
8877 Jefferson Paige Rd.
Shreveport, LA 71119
Tel: 318-938-5402

Hodges Gardens
Highway 71, Box 900
Many, LA 71449
Tel: 800-354-3523

MARYLAND

Ladew Topiary Garden
3535 Jarrettsville Pike
Monkton, MD 21111
Tel: 410-557-9570

William Paca House & Garden
1 Martin St.
Annapolis, MD 21401
Tel: 410-267-6656

MASSACHUSETTS

Arnold Arboretum
125 Arborway
Cambridge, MA 02130
Tel: 617-524-1717

MICHIGAN

Dow Gardens
1018 W. Main St.
Midland, MI 48640
Tel: 517-631-2677

Matthai Botanical Gardens
University of Michigan
1800 Dixboro
Ann Arbor, MI 48109
Tel: 313-998-7061

MISSISSIPPI

Mynelle Gardens
4736 Clinton Blvd.
Jackson, MS 39209
Tel: 601-960-1894

NEW JERSEY

Duke Gardens Foundation
Route 206
Somerville, NJ 08876
Tel: 908-722-3700

Frelinghuysen Arboretum
53 E. Hanover Ave.
Morristown, NJ 07960
Tel: 201-326-7600

NEW YORK

Boscobel
Route 9D
Garrison, NY 10524
Tel: 914-265-3638

Brooklyn Botanic Garden
Cranford Rose Garden
1000 Washington Ave.
Brooklyn, NY 11225
Tel: 718-622-4433

The Cloisters
Fort Tryon Park
New York, NY 10040
Tel: 212-923-3700

**Franklin D. Roosevelt
Garden**
Route 9
Hyde Park, NY 12538
Tel: 914-229-8114

New York Botanical Garden
Peggy Rockefeller Rose
Garden
200 St. & Kazimiroff Blvd.
Bronx, NY 10458
Tel: 718-817-8700

Old Westbury Gardens
710 Old Westbury Rd.
Old Westbury, NY 11568
Tel: 516-333-0048

**Vanderbilt Mansion &
Gardens**
Route 9
Hyde Park, NY 12538
Tel: 914-229-7770

Wave Hill
675 W. 252nd St.
Bronx, NY 10471
Tel: 718-549-3200

NORTH CAROLINA

Biltmore Estate
1 North Park Sq.
Asheville, NC 28801
Tel: 800-543-2961

OKLAHOMA

Woodard Park Garden
2435 S. Peoria
Tulsa, OK 74114
Tel: 918-746-5425

OREGON

**Washington Park
International Rose Test
Garden**
Washington Park
Portland, OR 97201
Tel: 503-823-3636

PENNSYLVANIA

Longwood Gardens
U.S. 1, P.O. Box 501
Kennett Square, PA 19348
Tel: 610-388-6741

SOUTH CAROLINA

Magnolia Plantation & Gardens
Highway 61
Charleston, SC 29407
Tel: 803-571-1266

Middleton Place
Highway 61
Charleston, SC 29407
Tel: 800-782-3608

TENNESSEE

Cheekwood
1200 Forrest Park Dr.
Nashville, TN 37205
Tel: 615-356-8000

TEXAS

Dallas Arboretum & Botanical Garden
8525 Garland Rd.
Dallas, TX 75218
Tel: 214-327-8263

VIRGINIA

Bon-Air Memorial Rose Garden
Wilson Blvd. & Lexington St.
Arlington, VA 22201
Tel: 703-358-3317

Monticello
P.O. Box 316, Route 53
Charlottesville, VA 22902
Tel: 804-984-9822

Mt. Vernon
Mt. Vernon, VA 22121
Tel: 703-780-2000

Woodlawn Plantation Period Rose Garden
9000 Richmond Highway
Alexandria, VA 22121
Tel: 703-780-4000

Don't Miss

OKLAHOMA

McBirney Mansion
1414 S. Galveston
Tulsa, OK 74127
Tel: 918-585-3234
Fax: 918-585-9377

A restored gem of an inn.

TENNESSEE

The Inn at Blackberry Farm
1471 W. Millers Cove Rd.
Walland, TN 37886
Tel: 423-984-8166
Fax: 423-983-5708

Set in an idyllic spot in the beautiful Smoky Mountains.

TEXAS

The Mansion at Turtle Creek
2821 Turtle Creek Blvd.
Dallas, TX 75219
Tel: 214-559-2100
Fax: 214-528-4187

Remarkable flowers and fine dining at this special hotel.

Some beautiful gardens in Britain. **CLOCKWISE, ABOVE RIGHT**: Powerscourt, one of the most impressive gardens in Ireland; a garden bench surrounded by roses and delphinium at Haddon Hall; the hotel terrace at Chewton Glen; Broughton Castle's neat parterres filled with lush plantings; an allee of *Rosa gallica* and *mundi* at Kiftsgate Court.

British Isles
The British are a nation of gardeners and there are probably more glorious gardens in Britain than anywhere. Even from a train window, you can see the carefully tended, colorful cottage gardens planted almost to the tracks! Needless to say, the ones listed here are more elegant, but no less charming, and filled with roses.

Gardens

ENGLAND

Barnsley House Garden
Barnsley, Near Cirencester
Gloucestershire GL7 5EE
Tel: 011-44-285-740281

Bateman's
Burwash, Etchingham
Sussex TN19 7DS
Tel: 011-44-435-882302

Blickling Hall
Blickling, Norwich
Norfolk NR11 6NF
Tel: 011-44-0263-733084

Broughton Castle
Near Banbury
Oxfordshire OX15 5EG
Tel: 011-44-295-262624

Castle Drogo
Drewsteignton
Devon EX6 6PB
Tel: 011-44-647-433306

Castle Howard
Near York
North Yorkshire YO6 7DA
Tel: 011-44-065-384333

Chartwell
Westerham
Kent TN16 1PS
Tel: 011-44-732-866368

Claverton Manor
Near Bath
Avon BA2 7BD
Tel: 011-44-225-460503

Cliveden
Taplow, Maidenhead
Berkshire SL6 0JA
Tel: 011-44-628-605069

Cotehele
St. Dominick, near Saltash
Cornwall PL12 6TA
Tel: 011-44-579-50434

Cranborne Manor Garden
Cranborne, near Wimborne
Dorset BH21 5PP
Tel: 011-44-725-517248

David Austin
Bowling Green Lane
Albrighton, Wolverhampton
West Midlands WV7 3HB
Tel: 011-44-902-373931

The Garden Bookshop
11 Blenheim Crescent
London W1
Tel: 011-44-171-792-0777
Fax: 011-44-171-792-1991

Considered one of the best in London.

**The General
Trading Company**
144 Sloane St.
London SW1
Tel: 011-44-171-730-0411

Flower power for home and garden in this wonderful store in a sprawling house.

The Lanesborough Hotel
Hyde Park Corner
London SW1X 7TA
Tel: 800-899-1828
011-44-171-259-5599
Fax: 011-44-171-259-5606

No luxurious detail is overlooked, including your very own butler.

Mrs. Monro
16 Motcomb St.
London SW1
Tel: 011-44-171-235-0326

A shop filled with roses on lovely china, needlepoint rugs and other unique antiques.

Emmetts Garden
Ide Hill, Sevenoaks
Kent TN14 6AY
Tel: 011-44-073-275367

Farnborough Hall
Banbury, Oxfordshire
Warwickshire OX17 1DU
Tel: 011-44-788-535555

Fenton House
Windmill Hill, Hampstead
London NW3 6RT
Tel: 011-44-071-4353471

Gawthorpe Hall
Padiham, near Burnley
Lancashire BB12 8UA
Tel: 011-44-282-78511

Gravetye Manor
Near East Grinstead
West Sussex RH19 4LJ
Tel: 011-44-342-810567

Great Dixter
Northiam, Rye
East Sussex TN31 6PH
Tel: 011-44-797-253160

Greys Court
Rotherfield Greys
Henley-on-Thames
Oxfordshire RG9 4PG
Tel: 011-44-049-17529

Gunby Hall
Gunby, near Spilsby
Lincolnshire PE23 5SS
Tel: 011-44-522-532424

Haddon Hall
Bakewell
Derbyshire DE4 1LA
Tel: 011-44-629-812855

Hardwick Hall
Doe Lea, Chesterfield
Derbyshire S44 5QJ
Tel: 011-44-246-850430

Hatfield House
Hatfield
Hertfordshire AL9 5NQ
Tel: 011-44-707-262823

Helmingham Hall
Near Stowemarket
Suffolk IP14 6EF
Tel: 011-44-01-473-890363

Hidcote Manor Garden
Hidcote Bartrim, near Chipping
Campden
Gloucestershire GL55 6LR
Tel: 011-44-386-438333

Hughenden Manor
High Wycombe
Buckinghamshire HP14 4LA
Tel: 011-44-494-532580

Kedleston Hall
Derby
Derbyshire DE6 4JN
Tel: 011-44-332-842191

Kiftsgate Court
Near Chipping Campden
Gloucestershire GL55 6LW
Tel: 011-44-386-438777

Lamb House
West Street, Rye
Sussex TN31 7ES
Tel: 011-44-424-433711

Lanhydrock
Bodmin
Cornwall PL30 5AD
Tel: 011-44-208-73320

Lyme Park
Disley, Stockport
Cheshire SK12 2NX
Tel: 011-44-663-762023

Mannington Hall
Norwich
Norfolk NR11 7BB
Tel: 011-44-026-387284

Montacute House
Montacute
Somerset TA15 6XP
Tel: 011-44-935-823289

Mottisfont Abbey Garden
Mottisfont, near Romsey
Hampshire SO51 0LJ
Tel: 011-44-794-41220

Nymans Garden
Handcross, near Haywards
Heath
Sussex RH17 6EB
Tel: 011-44-444-400321

Peckover House
North Brink, Wisbech
Cambridgeshire PE13 1JR
Tel: 011-44-945-583463

Polesden Lacey
Near Dorking
Surrey RH5 6BD
Tel: 011-44-372-458203

Gravetye Manor
Near East Grinstead
West Sussex RH19 4LJ
Tel: 011-44-01342-810567
Fax: 011-44-01342-810080

Stay in an Elizabethan house, with gardens designed by William Robinson.

DUBLIN

Hodges Figgis Bookstore
56/58 Dawson St.
Dublin
Tel: 011-353-1-6774754
Fax: 011-353-1-6792810

Ireland is famous for her outstanding bookstores, and this is one of the best.

Merrion Hotel
Upper Merrion St.
Dublin
Tel: 011-353-1-603-0600
Fax: 011-353-1-603-0700

Elegant Georgian hospitality surrounds you with chintzes, flowers and scented soaps.

**Restaurant
Patrick Guilbaud**
46 James Pl.
Dublin
Tel: 011-353-1-734192

This famous Irish chef's restaurant is next to the Merrion Hotel.

Queen Mary's Garden
Inner Circle, Regents Park
London NW1
Tel: 011-44-171-4867905

Royal Botanic Garden
Kew, Richmond
Surrey TW9 1BR
Tel: 011-44-181-9401171

Royal National Rose Society
Chiswell Green
Hertfordshire AL2 3NR
Tel: 011-44-727-850461

Rufford Old Hall
Rufford, near Ormskirk
Lancashire L40 1SG
Tel: 011-44-704-821254

Shugborough Estate
Milford, near Stafford
Staffordshire ST17 0XB
Tel: 011-44-889-881388

Sissinghurst Castle Garden
Sissinghurst, near Cranbrook
Kent TN17 2AB
Tel: 011-44-580-712850

Speke Hall
The Walk, Liverpool
Merseyside L24 1XD
Tel: 011-44-051-4277231

Tatton Park
Knutsford
Cheshire WA16 6QN
Tel: 011-44-565-654822

Upton House
Banbury, Oxfordshire
Warwickshire OX15 6HT
Tel: 011-44-295-87266

Wightwick Manor
Wightwick Bank
Wolverhampton
West Midlands WV6 8EE
Tel: 011-44-902-761108

Wimpole Hall
Arrington, Royston
Hertfordshire
Cambridgeshire SG8 0BW
Tel: 011-44-223-207257

Wisley Garden
Near Ripley, Woking
Surrey GU23 6QB
Tel: 011-44-483-224234

WALES

Bodnant Garden
Tal-y-Cafn, Colwyn Bay
Clwyd LL28 5RE
Tel: 011-44-492-650460

Chirk Castle
Chirk
Clwyd LL14 5AF
Tel: 011-44-691-777701

Powis Castle
Welshpool
Powys SY21 8RF
Tel: 011-44-938-554336

IRELAND & NORTHERN IRELAND

Altamont Gardens
Tullow, Co. Carlow
Tel: 011-353-503-59128

Ardress House
64 Ardress Rd.
Portadown, Co. Armagh
Northern Ireland
Tel: 011-44-1762-851236

Ballinlough Castle Gardens and Demesne
Clonmellon, Co. Westmeath
Tel: 011-353-46-33135

Butterstream Garden
Trim, Co. Meath
Tel: 011-353-46-36017
By appointment.

Graigueconna
Old Connaught Bray
Co. Wicklow
Tel: 011-353-1-282-2273

Hilton Park
Clones, Co. Monaghan
Tel: 011-353-47-56007

Mount Juliet
Thomastown, Co. Kilkenny
Tel: 011-353-056-24455

National Botanic Garden
Glasnevin, Dublin
Tel: 011-353-1-8377596

Powerscourt Gardens
Enniskerry, Co. Wicklow
Tel: 011-353-1-204-6000

Ram House Gardens
Coolgreany, Gorey,
Co. Wexford
Tel: 011-353-02-37238

Don't Miss

IRISH COUNTRYSIDE

Ballymaloe House
Shangarry, Co. Cork
Tel: 011-353-21-652531

You can take cooking lessons, browse in the shop, stroll in the gardens, and smell the pink Ballymaloe rose, all while staying in this charming hotel.

The Berkeley Costume & Toy Museum
Berkeley Forest
New Ross, Co. Wexford
Tel: 011-353-1-421361

A private collection of antique costumes, dolls and toys in a magnificent Georgian home. By appointment.

Longueville House
Mallow, Co. Cork
Tel: 011-353-22-47156

The produce for the wonderful meals served in this hotel is grown in their own gardens and greenhouses.

Marlfield House
Courtown Rd.
Gorey, Co. Wexford
Tel: 011-353-55-21124

A luxurious Regency mansion hotel surrounded by 36 acres of elegant gardens filled with thousands of roses.

Roses blooming in France.
CLOCKWISE, ABOVE RIGHT:
the sign to the rose garden
at Château de la Mes-
sardière; the entrance of
Monet's home in Giverny;
the Jardin Ephrussi de
Rothschild, a Venetian
palazzo and rose gardens;
a bouquet at the Hotel Le
Bristol in Paris; and the
magnificent June roses at
the Parc de Bagatelle in
Paris.

ROSERAIE

France

If you have the opportunity, a visit to France when all the roses are in bloom is a rare treat. Depending on the weather, this usually occurs in late May and June. Northern or southern France, it doesn't matter, because the roses are the lushest you'll ever see.

Gardens

Le Bois des Moutiers
Varengeville-sur-Mer 76119
Tel: 011-33-2-35-85-10-02

La Bonne Maison
99 chemin de Fontanières
La Mulatière-Lyon,
Rhône 69350
Tel: 011-33-78-42-42-82

Château d'Ainay-Le-Vieil
Ainay-Le-Vieil
Cher 18200
Tel: 011-33-48-63-50-67

Château de Bagnols
Bagnols, Rhône 69620
Tel: 011-33-74-71-40-00

Château de Beauregard
Chens-sur-Leman
The-Savoie 74140
Tel: 011-33-50-94-04-07

Château de Malmaison
1 avenue du Château
Reur Malmaison 92500
Tel: 011-33-1-41-29-05-55

Château de Pin
Champ Tocé-sur-Loire 49170
Tel: 011-33-2-41-39-91-85

Château de Vignal
Rte de Berre-les-Alpes
Contes 06390
Tel: 011-33-93-79-00-11

Don't Miss

Whenever I go to the gardens listed here, I try to visit these wonderful spots.

PARIS

Comoglio
22 rue Jacob
Paris 75006
Tel: 011-33-1-43-54-65-86
Fax: 011-33-1-40-51-70-56

I love their copies of antique fabrics with floral themes.

Hotel Le Bristol
112 rue du Faubourg
St. Honoré
Paris 75008
Tel: 011-33-1-53-43-43-00
Fax: 011-33-1-53-43-43-01

The most beautiful interior hotel garden in the city.

La Maison Rustique
26 rue Jacob
Paris 75006
Tel: 011-33-1-42-34-96-60
Fax: 011-33-1-42-34-96-62

Handsome flower and garden books on one of my favorite streets.

L'Orangerie
28 rue St. Louis-en-l'Isle
Paris 75004
Tel: 011-33-1-46-33-93-98

Audrey Hepburn's favorite— the prettiest flower-filled restaurant.

SOUTH OF FRANCE

**Château de la
Chèvre d'Or**
Eze-Village 06360
Tel: 011-33-04-92-10-66-66
Fax: 011-33-04-93-41-06-72

*Stay in this lovely hotel for
incredible views and hilltops
planted with roses.*

**Le Château du Domaine
St. Martin**
Ave des Templiers
Vence 06140
Tel: 011-33-04-93-58-02-02
Fax: 011-33-4-93-24-08-91

*Visit this extraordinary hotel
in June, when the roses are
all in bloom.*

Château de la Messardière
Route de Tahiti
St. Tropez 83990
Tel: 011-33-4-94-56-76-00
Fax: 011-33-4-94-56-76-01

*Enjoy lush landscaped
gardens by the sea from your
hotel terrace.*

**Gaec Pepinières, Côte-Sud-
des-Landes**
St. Geours-de-Maremme
Landes 40230
Tel: 011-33-58-57-33-30

Jardin Bossuet
5 Place Charles de Gaulle
Meaux 77100
Tel: 011-33-1-64-34-84-45

Jardin Curé Claude Pigeard
Musée de l'Outil
Wy-dit-Joli-Village
Val d'Oise 95420
Tel: 011-33-34-67-41-79

**Jardin des Cinq Sens
Labyrinthe**
Rue du Lac
Yvoire, Haut-Savoie 74140
Tel: 011-33-50-72-88-80

**Jardin Ephrussi
de Rothschild**
Ave Ephrussi de Rothschild
St. Jean-Cap-Ferrat 06230
Tel: 011-33-93-01-33-09

Jardins Albert Kahn
14 rue du Port
Boulogne-Billancourt
Hauts-de-Seine 92100
Tel: 011-33-47-12-02-44

Jardins Claude Monet
Musée Claude Monet
Giverny, Eure 27620
Tel: 011-33-32-51-28-21

Les Jardins d'Angélique
Montmaim 76520
Seine-Maritime 76520
Tel: 011-33-35-79-08-12

Les Jardins de L'Imaginaire
Terrasson-la-Villedieu
Dordogne 24120
Tel: 011-33-53 50-37-56

Les Jardins de Villandry
Villandry, Indre-et-Loire 37510
Tel: 011-33-47-50-02-09

Jourdan et Eve
Le Chesnoy
Treilles, Loiret 45490
Tel: 011-33-38-87-83-58

Parc de Bagatelle
Bois de Boulogne
Rte de Severes à Neuilly
Paris 75016
Tel: 011-33-1-45-01-20-50

Parc de la Tête d'Or
Place Leclerc
Lyon 69459
Tel: 011-33-4-78-89-53-52

Roseraie de Berty
Largentière, Ardèche 07110
Tel: 011-33-75-88-30-56
By appointment only.

Roseraie de l'Hay les Roses
1 rue Albert Watel
L'Hay les Roses 94240
Tel: 011-33-1-47-40-04-04

Roseraies P. Guillot
Domaine de la Plaine
Chamagnieu, Isère 38460
Tel: 011-33-74 90 27 55

Serre de la Madone
74 Arte de Gorbio
Menton 06500
Tel: 011-33-93-28-29-1

Don't Miss

**Fragonard Parfumerie
& Musée**
20 bd Fragonard
Grasse 06332
Tel: 011-33-4-93-36-44-65
Fax: 011-33-4-93-36-03-50

*Buy rose soaps and bath oils
in the shop, then visit the
museum filled with antique
perfume treasures.*

Hotel Imperial Garoupe
770 chemin de la Garoupe
Cap d'Antibes 06600
Tel: 011-33-4-92-93-31-61
Fax: 011-33-4-92-93-31-62

*Visit the beach that F. Scott
Fitzgerald made famous.*

Moulin de Mougins
Notre Dame de Vie
Mougins 06250
Tel: 011-33-4-93-75-78-24
Fax: 011-33-4-93-90-18-55

*Dine in Roger Vergé's secluded
flower-filled restaurant.*

Take a walk in one of these grand gardens. **CLOCKWISE, ABOVE RIGHT:** a hidden gem on Lake Como is Villa Monastero; either way you go, the gardens are beautiful; the fountain at the Villa Carlotta in Tremezzo; terraced gardens stretch to the lake at the Rockefeller Villa Serbelloni; a lavender-edged walkway in Ninfa, a magical garden south of Rome.

AI GIARDINI

Italy

The gardens of Italy are unique in that they revolve around architectural elements. In many cases flowers are not the focal point, but you'll find roses that will interest you in many of these gardens and you will leave with fresh ideas for your own.

Gardens

American Academy in Rome
5 Via Angelo Masina
Rome 00153
Tel: 011-39-6-584-61

Bomarzo
Sacro Bosco
Bomarzo 01020
Tel: 011-39-761-924-029

Borghese Gallery
Piazzale Scipione Borghese
Rome 00197
Tel: 011-39-6-854-8577

Castello Ruspoli
9 Piazza della Repubblica
Vignanello 01039
Tel: 011-39-6-6876147

Giardini Botanici Hanbury
43 Via Monte Carlo
La Mortola 18030
Tel: 011-39-18-42-29-852

Giardini della Landriana
Tor San Lorenzo
51 Via Campo di Carne
Ardea 00186
Tel: 011-39-6-91-01-03-50

Giardino Garzoni
Piazza della Vittoria
Collodi 51014
Tel: 011-39-572-429131

Giusti Gardens
2 Via Giardino Giusti
Verona 37129
Tel: 011-39-45-803-4029

Ninfa
Via Ninfina
Doganella di Ninfa 04010
For tickets to visit: Fondazione
Roffreddo Caetani
Tel: 011-39-6-688-032-31

Orto Botanico
24 Largo Cristina di Svezia
Rome 00165
Tel: 011-39-6-686-4193

Palazzo Corsini
58 Via Il Prato
Florence 50123
Tel: 011-39-55-218994

The Vatican Gardens
Piazza San Pietro
Città del Vaticano
Rome 00120
Tel: 011-39-6-698-844-66

Don't Miss

Whenever I go to the gardens listed here, I try to visit these wonderful spots.

ROME

Campo dei Fiori
Near the Piazza Navona
Mon.–Sat. 6 A.M. to 1 P.M.

Be sure to visit this outdoor flower market.

The Hassler Hotel
6 Piazza Trinità dei Monti
Rome 00187
Tel: 011-39-6-699-340
Fax: 011-39-6-678-999

Stay here and have a drink in the delightful Palm Court.

La Posta Vecchia
Palo Laziale
Ladispoli 00050
Tel: 011-39-06-994-9501

J. Paul Getty's home above Rome, now a beautiful hotel.

FLORENCE

Farmacia di Santa Maria Novella
16 Via della Scala
Florence 50123
Tel: 011-39-55-21-62-76

A convent from 1612 now sells rose water and other elegant toiletries.

Grand Hotel
1 Piazza Ognissanti
Florence 50123
Tel: 011-39-55-288781
Fax: 011-39-55-217400

Have an aperitif in the turn-of-the-century winter garden.

VENICE

Locanda Cipriani
Torcello 30012
Tel: 011-39-41-73-01-50
Fax: 011-39-41-73-54-33

Eat lunch on this tranquil island in the midst of flower and vegetable gardens.

LAKE COMO

Restaurant Isola Comacina
Comacina, Lake Como
22010
Tel: 011-39-344-55083

The perfect spot for a long lunch after garden-hopping around the lake.

Villa d'Este Grand Hotel
40 Via Regina
Cernobbio, Lake Como
22012
Tel: 011-39-31-511-471
Fax: 011-39-31-348-844

Spectacular gardens—a must-see.

Villa Carlotta
2 Via Regina
Tremezzo, Lake Como 22019
Tel: 011-39-344-40405

Villa del Balbianello
Lenno, Lake Como 22016
Tel: 011-39-344-56110

Villa d'Este
1 Piazza Trento
Tivoli 00019
Tel: 011-39-774-312-070

Villa Gamberaia
72 Via del Rossellino
Settignano 50135
Tel: 011-39-55-697205

Villa Giulia
9 Piazzale di Villa Giulia
Rome 00196
Tel: 011-39-6-322-6571

Villa Lante
71 Via J. Barozzi
Bagnaia 01031
Tel: 011-39-761-288-008

Villa Marlia
Via Villa Reale
Marlia 55014
Tel: 011-39-583-30108

Villa Melzi D'Eril
Via Lago
Bellagio, Lake Como 22021
Tel: 011-39-31-950318

Villa Monastero
2 Via Polvani
Varenna, Lake Como 22050
Tel: 011-39-341-830129

Villa Serbelloni
Rockefeller Gardens
Via Garibaldi
Bellagio, Lake Como 22021
Tel: 011-39-31-950105

Villa Trissino Marzotto
Piazza Gian Giorgio Trissino
Trissino 36070
Tel: 011-39-445-962029

Germany and Austria

Germany has some very beautiful rose gardens. One of the prettiest is in Baden-Baden, a charming town where you can relax, visit some of the best spas in the world and smell the roses. Austrian gardens, though formally designed, have an abundance of charm, and of roses.

Gardens

GERMANY

Kurpark and Lichentaleralee
Baden-Baden 76530
Tel: 011-49-7221-275200

Rosarium Sangerhausen
Steinberger Weg 3
Sangerhausen 06526
Tel: 011-49-3464-572522

AUSTRIA

Mirabell Gardens
Mirabellplatz
Salzburg

Schonbrunn Palace Gardens
13 Schonbrunner
Schlosstrasse
Vienna 1130
Tel: 011-43-1-83-36-46

Volksgarten
Dr. Karl Renner Ring
Vienna 1010

SOURCE GUIDE

Insider Garden Tours

Visiting a garden with someone "in the know" can be a very special experience. In some cases you will be going to gardens that are rarely, if ever, open to the public.

ENGLAND

Expo Garden Tours
70 Great Oak Lane
Redding, CT 06896
Tel: 800-448-2685
Fax: 203-938-0427

Escorted tours of gardens around the world, with an emphasis on those in Britain.

The Garden Party
Owner: Patty Floyd
Great Chalfield Manor
Melksham
Wiltshire SN12 8NJ
England
Tel: 011-44-1225-782239
Fax: 011-44-1225-783379

Tours of gardens and manor houses in England.

FRANCE

Louisa Jones
Rousselonge
Payzac 07230, France
Tel: 011-33-04-75-39-48-31
Fax: 011-33-04-75-39-99-29

Specialists in visiting gardens in Provence and the countryside.

Serenoa Conseil
Owner: Maria Claude-Letang
9 Bd de Rothschild
Grasse 06130, France
Tel/Fax: 011-33-4-93-36-58-04

Tours of the special gardens on the French and Italian Riviera.

ITALY

Grandi Giardini Italiani
7 Piazza Cavour
Cabiate 22060, Italy
Tel: 011-39-31-75-67-69-71

Tours of Italian gardens.

NEW ZEALAND

J. Barry Ferguson
P.O. Box 176
Oyster Bay, NY 11771
Tel: 516-922-0005

A special look at beautiful rose gardens "down under."

Favorite Books

Austin, David. *English Roses.* London: Conran Octopus, 1993.

Beales, Peter. *Classic Roses.* London: Collins Harville, 1985.

Browne, Jim with William J. Radler and Nelson W. Stern. *Rose Gardening.* New York: Pantheon, 1995.

Bunyard, E.A. *Old Garden Roses.* London: Country Life, 1936.

Gault, S. Miller and Patrick M. Synge. *The Dictionary of Roses in Colour.* London: Michael Joseph Ltd., 1985.

Griffiths, Trevor. *The Book of Old Roses.* London: Michael Joseph Ltd., Mermaid Books, 1984.

Jekyll, Gertrude and Edward Mawley. *Roses for English Gardens.* New York: Penguin Books, 1983.

Keays, Mrs. E.E. *Old Roses.* New York: Macmillan, 1935.

Page, Russell. *The Education of a Gardener.* New York: Random House, 1983.

Perenyi, Eleanor. *Green Thoughts.* New York: Vintage Books, 1983.

Princess Grace of Monaco. *My Book of Flowers.* New York: Doubleday, 1980.

Reddell, Rayford Clayton. *The Rose Bible.* New York: Harmony Books, 1994.

Sackville-West, Vita. *A Joy of Gardening.* New York: Harper & Row, 1958.

——. *Garden Book.* Slough, Bucks: Holland Sweet Press, Ltd., 1998.

——. *In Your Garden.* London: Michael Joseph Ltd., 1951.

Sitwell, Sacheverell, Wilfred Blunt, and John Russell. *Old Garden Roses.* London: George Rainbird, 1955–57, two vols.

Spry, Constance. *Flowers in House & Garden.* New York: G. P. Putnam, 1937.

Stemler, Dorothy. *Book of Old Roses.* Boston: Bruce Humphries, 1966.

Thomas, Graham Stuart. *Old Shrub Roses.* London: J. M. Dent & Sons, 1955.

Verey, Rosemary. *The Scented Garden.* New York: Van Nostrand Reinhold, 1981.

Organizations & Associations

There is nothing better than networking with people who have the same interests as you do. If you join any of these organizations, you will have the opportunity to attend interesting lectures and meet people who also love beautiful roses, homes and gardens.

UNITED STATES

American Horticultural Society
7931 E. Boulevard Dr.
Alexandria, VA 22308
Tel: 703-768-5700

American Rose Society
P.O. Box 30000
Shreveport, LA 71130
Tel: 800-637-6534

Friends of Vieilles Maisons Françaises
180 Maiden Lane
New York, NY 10038
Tel: 212-734-1651

Garden Club of America
598 Madison Ave.
New York, NY 10022
Tel: 212-753-8287

The Garden Conservancy
Box 219
Cold Spring, NY 10516
Tel: 914-265-2029

Heritage Rose Foundation
1512 Gorman St.
Raleigh, NC 27606

Horticultural Society of New York
128 W. 58th St.
New York, NY 10019
Tel: 212-757-0915

The Irish Georgian Society
7 Washington Square N.
New York, NY 10012
Tel: 212-759-7155

The Royal Oak Foundation
285 W. Broadway, Suite 400
New York, NY 10013
Tel: 212-966-6565

CANADA

Canadian Rose Society
c/o Anne Graber
10 Fairfax Crescent
Scarborough, Ontario M1L 1Z8
Tel: 416-757-8809

ENGLAND

The National Garden Scheme
57 Lower Belgrave St.
London SW1W 0LR
Tel: 011-44-171-730-0359

National Trust
Membership Department
P.O. Box 39
Bromley, Kent BR1 3XL
Tel: 011-44-181-315-1111

Royal Horticultural Society
80 Vincent Sq.
London SW1P 2PE
If you join, you can obtain tickets to the famous Chelsea Flower Show by contacting their Membership Department:
P.O. Box 313
London SW1P 2PE
Tel: 011-44-171-821-3000

The Royal National Rose Society
Chiswell Green
St. Albans
Hertfordshire AL2 3N4
Tel: 011-44-01-727-850461

AUSTRALIA

National Rose Society
271B Belmore Rd.
North Balwin, Vic 3104

Supplies

Here are some of the places where you can find the special materials used in the projects in this book.

Essential Rose Oils

- **Kiehl's**
  109 Third Ave.
  New York, NY 10003
  Tel: 800-543-4571
  Fax: 212-505-1023
  Free catalogue.

- **Cherchez Mail Order**
  P.O. Box 550
  Millbrook, NY 12545
  Tel: 800-422-1744

Beeswax Pellets, Cosmetic Jars and Glass Vinegar Bottles

- **Johnny's Selected Seeds**
  Foss Hill Road
  RR1, Box 2580
  Albion, ME 04910
  Tel: 207-437-4301
  Fax: 800-437-4290
  Free catalogue.

Wreath Forms

- **Frank's Nursery & Crafts**
  6501 E. Nevada
  Detroit, MI 48234
  Tel: 313-366-8400 (call for nearest store)

Silk Flowers

- **K and D Flowers**
  46 Graphic Place
  Moonachie, NJ 07074
  800-543-NYNY
  Showroom open to trade and public. Full color catalogue, $10 (refunded with purchase).

Dried Botanicals for Arranging

- **Meadows Direct**
  13805 Highway 136
  Onslow, IA 53231
  Tel: 800-542-9771
  Fax: 319-485-2725
  Catalogue, $6.55 ppd

Dried Botanicals for Making Potpourri

- **Aphrodisia**
  264 Bleeker St.
  New York, NY 10014
  Tel: 212-989-6440
  Fax: 212-989-8027

- **Cherchez Mail Order**
  P.O. Box 550
  Millbrook, NY 12545
  800-422-1744

Silk Fabric

- **Scalamandré**
  942 Third Ave.
  New York, NY 10022
  Tel: 212-980-3888
  Fax: 212-688-7531
  Showroom to the trade.

Rose Gloves, Aqua-Blum, Silica Gel, and Cutting Tools

- **Dorothy Biddle**
  348 Greeley Lake Rd.
  Greeley, PA 18425
  Tel: 570-226-3239
  Fax: 570-226-0349
  Free catalogue.

Cutting Tools and Rose-Related Items

- **Gardener's Eden**
  1000 Covington Cross
  Las Vegas, NV 89134
  Tel: 800-822-9600
  Fax: 702-360-7091

- **Smith and Hawken**
  P.O. Box 6900
  Florence, KY 41022
  Tel: 800-776-3336
  Fax: 606-727-1166

Freeze-Dried Roses

- **Flowers From Secret Gardens**
  184 S. Lake Forest Dr.
  McKinney, TX 75070
  Tel: 972-540-5300
  Fax: 972-540-5303

Pesticide-Free Rose Petals

- **Grace's Marketplace**
  1237 Third Ave.
  New York, NY 10021
  Tel: 888-Graces-1
  Fax: 212-861-7420

Rose Catalogues

You can order all kinds of roses, including old-fashioned shrub and other rare or miniature roses, from these special nurseries. Remember to inquire about permits needed to import any roses from England to the United States.

UNITED STATES

Antique Rose Emporium
Rte. 5, Box 143
Brenham, TX 77833
Tel: 409-836-9051

Arena Rose Co.
P.O. Box 3096
Paso Robles, CA 93447
Tel: 805-227-4094

Armstrong Roses
P.O. Box 4220
Huntington Sta., NY 11746
Tel: 800-321-6640

Blossoms & Bloomers
E. 11415 Krueger Lane
Spokane, WA 99207
Tel: 509-922-1344

Heirloom Old Garden Roses
24062 N.E. Riverside Dr.
St. Paul, OR 97137
Tel: 505-538-1576

High County Rosarium
1717 Downing
Denver, CO 80218
Tel: 303-832-4026

Jackson & Perkins
1 Rose Lane
Medford, OR 97501
Tel: 800-292-4769

La Loma Roses
P.O. Box 772
Somis, CA 93066
Tel: 805-386-8002

Limberlost Roses
7304 Forbes Ave.
Van Nuys, CA 91406
Tel: 818-901-7798

Lowe's Own-Root Roses
6 Sheffield Rd.
Nashua, NH 03062
Tel: 603-888-2214

Pixie Treasures
4121 Prospect Ave.
Yorba Linda, CA 92686
Tel: 714-993-6780

Roses by Fred Edmunds
6235 S.W. Kahle Rd.
Wilsonville, OR 97070
Tel: 503-638-4671

Roses of Yesterday & Today
802 Brown's Valley Rd.
Watsonville, CA 95076
Tel: 408-724-2755

Vintage Gardens
2833 Old Gravenstein Hwy.
South
Sebastopol, CA 95472
Tel: 707-829-2035
Fax: 707-829-9516

Wayside Gardens
Box 1
Hodges, SC 29695
Tel: 800-845-1124

White Flower Farm
P.O. Box 50
Litchfield, CT 06759
Tel: 800-888-7756

CANADA

J.C. Baker & Sons
RR3
St. Catherines
Ontario L2R 6P9
Tel: 905-935-4533

Old Rose Nursery
Central Rose
Hornby Island
British Columbia V0R 1Z0
Tel: 604-335-2603

Pickering Nurseries
670 Kingston Rd.
Pickering
Ontario L1V 1A6
Tel: 807-839-2111

ENGLAND

David Austin Roses
Bowling Green Lane
Albrighton, Wolverhampton
West Midlands, WV7 3HB
Tel: 011-44-01902-373931
Fax: 011-44-01902-372142

Peter Beales Roses
London Rd.
Attleborough
Norfolk NR17 1AY
Tel: 011-44-01953-454707
Fax: 011-44-01953-456845

INDEX

I wonder what it would be like

to live in a world where it was always June.

E. M. Montgomery